The Origin of the Bible

Here are some other useful books
in the *Quiknotes* series.
Add them to your library of
quick-reference books, today:

Quiknotes: The Books of the Bible
Quiknotes: The Books of the New Testament
Quiknotes: The Books of the Old Testament
Quiknotes: English Bible Versions
Quiknotes: Christian Classics

Quiknotes™

THE ORIGIN
OF THE
BIBLE

Philip W. Comfort, Ph.D.

Tyndale House Publishers, Inc.
WHEATON, ILLINOIS

Visit Tyndale's exciting Web site at www.tyndale.com

Edited by David P. Barrett

Library of Congress Cataloging-in-Publication Data

Comfort, Philip Wesley.
  The origin of the Bible / Philip Wesley Comfort.
    p. cm — (Quiknotes)
  Includes bibliographical references.
  ISBN 0-8423-3555-2 (softcover : alk. paper)
  1. Bible—History. 2. Bible—Versions—History. I. Title. II. Quiknotes (Wheaton, Ill.)
BS445.C655 2000
220.1—dc21   99-051648

Printed in the United States of America

06 05 04 03 02 01 00
8   7   6   5   4   3   2   1

CONTENTS

Introduction   vii
The Divine Origin of the Bible   1
How We Got the Old Testament   9
How We Got the New Testament   27
Ancient Versions of the Bible   53
English Versions of the Bible   61
Timeline of Events   75
For Further Reading   77

INTRODUCTION

Nearly everyone has heard of Darwin's *The Origin of Species,* especially since it is taught in most American schools. But very few people know about the origin of the Bible. Anyone who wants to study the Bible should know how it originated and how it has been handed down to us during the past three thousand years.

In this book we will take a journey from the original texts to the most recent English versions. This journey will include the ancient Hebrew texts of the Old Testament and Greek texts of the New Testament, the many manuscript copies of both testaments (including the exciting Dead Sea Scrolls discovered at Qumran and the discoveries of New Testament fragments in Egypt), and the making of many translations—especially in English. You don't need to know Hebrew or Greek to go on this journey. You only need an English Bible—and a desire to know its amazing origins.

The first chapter ("The Divine Origin of the Bible") focuses on how the writers of the Bible were divinely inspired to compose the various sections of the Bible. The second chapter ("How We Got the Old Testament") reveals the processes that

went into selecting the thirty-nine books of the Old Testament
and then provides a survey of the various manuscripts of the Old
Testament. The third chapter ("How We Got the New Testament") reveals the processes that went into selecting the twenty-
seven books of the New Testament and then provides a survey of
the various manuscripts of the New Testament. The fourth chapter ("Ancient Versions of the Bible") gives some history of the
earliest versions of the Bible. The fifth chapter ("English Versions of the Bible") gives a short explanation of translation philosophy and a summary of the many English Bibles that have
been made.

The Divine Origin
of the Bible

Christians are people of the Book. They love the Book, they live the Book, and they know the Book. But they can never love it, live it, and know it enough, because this Book is about God and about how people can know and experience God through Jesus Christ and his Spirit. This Book is the Book of books, the Bible.

How did we get this amazing Book, the Bible? This chapter explains how.

THE MESSAGE OF THE BIBLE

The word *Bible* comes from the Greek word *biblia* (books). The word is used for the collection of books regarded as Holy Scripture for Christians.

The Bible is composed of two main sections, the Old Testament and the New Testament. The word *testament* means "covenant" or "agreement." The Old Testament (or covenant) refers to the relationship that God established with his people, the Israelites, through Abraham and Moses. Part of this relationship involved a set of laws (often called simply "the Law") that his people were to obey. God promised to bless his people if they kept these laws, or commandments. But God's people were unable to keep the Law perfectly and continually broke the covenant, since they, like all people, were sinful. So God told his people through some of his prophets that he would establish a new covenant—one in which he would write his laws not on stone tablets (as he had done with the Ten Commandments) but on the very hearts of men and women (see Jeremiah 31:31-34; Hebrews 8:8-12). This new covenant became a reality when God's Son, Jesus Christ, came to earth. Through his death on the cross, which paid for everyone's failure to keep the terms of the old covenant, Jesus enabled everyone who believed to enter into this new covenant with God. All who participate in the new covenant believe that Jesus is the Son of God, and that he died on the cross to pay for their sins and rose from the dead to give them new life. So the books of the Old Testament focus on the old covenant between God and his people. The books of the New Testament focus on God's new covenant with every believer.

The Old Testament and New Testament are two parts of one divine revelation. The Old Testament begins with man and woman in the first paradise on earth; the New Testament concludes with a vision of a new heaven and a new earth. The Old Testament portrays humanity as fallen from a sinless condition and separated from God; the New Testament tells how believers are restored to favor through the sacrifice of Christ. The Old Testament predicts a coming Redeemer who will rescue men and women from eternal condemnation; the New Testament reveals the Christ who brought this salvation. In most of the Old Testament, the spotlight focuses on a sacrificial system in which the blood of animals provided a temporary handling of the sin problem; in the New Testament, Christ appears as the one who came to put an end to all sacrifice—to be himself the supreme sacrifice. In the Old Testament, numerous predictions foretell a coming Messiah who would save his people; in the New Testament, scores of passages detail how those prophecies were fulfilled in every way in Jesus Christ, the "descendant of King David and of Abraham" (Matthew 1:1). As Augustine said more than fifteen hundred years ago, "The New is in the Old contained; the Old is in the New explained."

THE INSPIRATION OF THE BIBLE

Writers often speak of being "inspired" to write their books, but of all the millions of books in the world, there is only one that was truly inspired by God. This amazing, divinely written book tells the wonderful story of God's love for humanity and his plan to redeem them from sin and destruction. But there is another amazing story—the story of how the Bible came to us.

The Bible was originally written in the ancient languages of Hebrew, Aramaic (a sister language of Hebrew), and Greek. As we mentioned, the writers of the Bible were inspired by God, meaning that God gave them the messages they wrote. The Bible itself tells us that it is an inspired text: "All Scripture is inspired by God" (2 Timothy 3:16). Literally, the word rendered *inspired* here is "God-breathed." In other words, every word of the Bible was breathed out from God and written by people. The apostle Peter affirmed this when he said that "no prophecy in Scripture ever came from the prophets themselves or because they wanted to prophesy. It was the Holy Spirit who moved the prophets to speak from God" (2 Peter 1:20-21).

It was the Holy Spirit who moved the prophets to speak from God. This short sentence is the key to understanding how the Bible came into being. Thousands of years ago, God chose certain people—such as Moses, David, Isaiah, Jeremiah, Ezekiel, and Daniel—to receive his words and write them down. What they wrote became books, or sections, of the Old Testament. Nearly two thousand years ago, God chose other men—such as Matthew, Mark, Luke, John, and Paul—to communicate his new message, the message of salvation through Jesus Christ. What they wrote became books, or sections, of the New Testament.

God gave his words to these men in many different ways. Certain writers of the Old Testament received messages directly from God. Moses was given the Ten Commandments inscribed on a stone when he was in God's presence on Mount Sinai. When David was composing his psalms to God, he received divine inspiration to foretell certain events that would occur a thousand years later in Jesus Christ's life. God told his prophets—such as Isaiah and Jeremiah—exactly what to say. Therefore, when they gave a message, it was God's words, not their own. This is why many Old Testament prophets often said, "This is what the Lord says." (This statement appears over two thousand times in the Old Testament.) To other prophets, such as Ezekiel and Daniel, God communicated his message through visions and dreams. They recorded exactly what they saw, whether they understood it or not. And other Old Testament writers, such as Samuel and Ezra, were directed by God to record events in the history of Israel.

Four hundred years after the last book of the Old Testament (Malachi) was written, God's Son, Jesus Christ, came to earth. In his teachings, he affirmed the divine authorship of the Old Testament writings (see Matthew 5:17-19; Luke 16:17; John 10:35). Furthermore, he often pointed to certain passages in the Old Testament as having predicted certain events in his life (see Luke 24:27, 44). The New Testament writers also affirmed the divine inspiration of the Old Testament text. It was the apostle Paul who was directed by God to write, "All Scripture is inspired by God" (2 Timothy 3:16). Quite specifically, he was speaking of the Old Testament. And, as was already noted, Peter said that the Old Testament prophets were motivated by the Holy Spirit to speak from God.

The New Testament is also God-inspired. Before Jesus left

this earth and returned to his Father, he told the disciples that he would send the Holy Spirit to them. He told them that one of the functions of the Holy Spirit would be to remind them of all the things that Jesus had said and then to guide them into all truth (see John 14:26; 15:26; 16:13-15). Those who wrote the Gospels were helped by the Holy Spirit to remember Jesus' exact words, and those who wrote other parts of the New Testament were guided by the Spirit as they wrote.

The inspiration for writing the Gospels didn't begin when the authors set pen to papyrus. The inspiration began when the disciples Matthew, Peter (for whom Mark wrote), and John were enlightened by their encounters with Jesus Christ, the Son of God. The apostles' experiences with him altered their lives forever, imprinting on their souls unforgettable images of the revealed God-man, Jesus Christ.

This is what John was speaking about in the prologue to his Gospel when he declared, "The Word became flesh and lived among us, and we have seen his glory" (1:14, NRSV). The "we" refers to those eyewitnesses of Jesus' glory—the apostles who lived with Jesus for over three years. John expands upon this reminiscence in the prologue to his first epistle, where he says, "We have heard him, touched him, seen him, and looked upon him" (1 John 1:1-2, paraphrased). In both the Gospel and the Epistle, the verbs are in the perfect tense, denoting a past action with a present, abiding effect. Those past encounters with Jesus were never forgotten by John; they lived with him and stayed with him as an inspiring spirit until the day—many years later—he wrote of them in his Gospel. The same could be said for Matthew and for Peter, who was really the author behind Mark's Gospel. Luke was not an eyewitness, but he based his Gospel on the accounts of those who were (see Luke 1:1-4).

The inspiration for the writing of the Epistles can also be traced to the writers' encounters with the living Christ. The most prominent epistle writer, Paul, repeatedly claims that his inspiration came from his encounter with the risen Christ (see, for example, 1 Corinthians 15:8-10). Peter also claims that his writings were based upon his experiences with the living Christ (see 1 Peter 5:1; 2 Peter 1:16-18). And so does John, who claims to have experienced the God-man visibly, audibly, and palpably (see 1 John 1:1-4)—both during the days of his ministry and after his resurrection. James and Jude make no such claim directly; but since they were the brothers of Jesus who became converts when they saw the risen Christ (this is certain for James— see 1 Corinthians 15:7—and presumed for Jude—see Acts 1:14), they, too, drew their inspiration from their encounters with the living Christ. Thus, all the writers of the New Testament letters (with the possible exception of the author of Hebrews, who is unknown) knew the living Christ. This is the relationship that qualified them to write the books that became part of the New Testament. This made them distinct from all others, no matter how good these other writings were.

The writers of the New Testament letters, or epistles, were also inspired by the Spirit when they wrote. Speaking for all the apostles, Paul indicated that the New Testament apostles were taught by the Holy Spirit what to say. The writers of the New Testament did not speak with "words of human wisdom," but with "words given to us by the Spirit" (see 1 Corinthians 2:10-13). For example, when the apostle John saw that Jesus Christ had come to give eternal life to people, the Spirit helped him express this truth in many different ways. Thus, the reader of John's Gospel sees different phrases about Jesus giving life: "Life itself was in him"; "It becomes a perpetual spring within them, giving them eternal life"; "I am the bread of life"; "you will have the light that leads to life"; "I am the resurrection and the life"; etc. (John 1:4; 4:14; 6:48; 8:12; 11:25). When the apostle Paul contemplated the fullness of Christ's deity, he was inspired by the Spirit to use such phrases as "the endless treasures available to them in Christ"; "In him lie hidden all the treasures of wisdom and knowledge"; "in Christ the fullness of God lives in a human body" (see Ephesians 3:8; Colossians 2:3; 2:9).

As the Spirit taught the writers, they used their own vocabulary and writing style to express the thought of the Spirit. As such, the Scriptures came as the result of divine and human cooperation. The Scriptures were not mechanically inspired—as if God used the writers as machines through whom he dictated the divine utterance. Rather, the Scriptures were inspired by God *and* written by people. The Bible, therefore, is both fully divine and fully human.

How We Got the Old Testament

. . . .

A Brief History of Israel

Before we list all the probable authors of the Old Testament, it will be helpful to briefly review Israelite history, since the Old Testament is essentially a record of God's dealings with these people.

The Israelites (whose physical descendants are now called Jews) trace their origin to a man named Abraham. God called Abraham's family to leave their polytheistic homeland in Mesopotamia (modern-day Iraq) and follow the Lord alone. In return, the Lord promised to bless Abraham, making him into a great nation (the Israelites). Through Abraham and his descendants the Lord also promised to bless the whole world.

Abraham obeyed God's call to follow him, as did his son Isaac and his grandson Jacob (later renamed Israel). God established a covenant (see the earlier explanation of "covenant" in the chapter "The Divine Origin of the Bible") with Abraham and his descendants, making them his chosen people, and he instructed them to circumcise all Israelite males as a sign of this covenant. God also promised to give Abraham's descendants the land of Canaan.

Before this happened, however, they would endure a time of slavery in Egypt.

The Israelites had originally entered Egypt as welcomed guests under the protection of Pharoah, but later they became enslaved by the Egyptians. When the time came for the Israelites to leave Egypt and claim their Promised Land, Canaan, God raised up a man named Moses, along with his brother, Aaron, to lead the way. At the Lord's direction, Moses confronted Pharaoh and told him to let God's people go. Pharaoh refused, bringing upon himself ten plagues from the Lord. After the tenth plague, which resulted in the death of all the firstborn males of Egypt (including Pharaoh's own son), Pharoah released the Israelites. This event, along with all that accompanied it (including the parting of the Red Sea) would later become the hallmark of the Lord's relationship with the Israelites. This is evidenced in the preamble to the Ten Commandments, which the Lord gave to the Israelites shortly after their release from Egypt: "I am the Lord your God, who rescued you from slavery in Egypt" (Exodus 20:2). The Ten Commandments, along with a long list of other requirements, were the code by which the Israelites were to live, and these were based upon the character of God himself.

As the Israelites neared the Promised Land, Moses sent twelve spies to investigate the new land. Ten of the spies returned with a fearful report, and the Israelites opted not to enter the land. The Lord was angry with his people for their lack of faith, so he caused them to wander in the wilderness for forty years before finally entering the Promised Land. Moses died just before the Israelites entered the Promised Land, and Joshua became their new leader.

Once the Israelites entered the Promised Land, they began the long process of conquering the many peoples who already lived there. Some of these peoples were never completely eliminated, and their pagan ways continued to exert influence among the Israelites throughout the nation's history. The Old Testament writers credited such paganism as the primary reason for the Exile, which is discussed below.

From the first few hundred years after the Israelites entered the Promised Land, they functioned essentially as a confederation of twelve tribes rather than as a unified nation. Local rulers, called judges, rose up from time to time to deliver the people from various oppressions and to lead them back to the Lord. Under Saul, however, all the tribes came under the rule of a single king. Due to his sinful actions, Saul did not pass on the kingdom to his children, and David became the new king. The Lord established a covenant with David, promising to establish his family as the eternal heirs to the throne. David was a very successful military strategist, and he vastly expanded Israel's domain. He also moved the capital to Jerusalem. After David, Solomon reigned as king, and God blessed him with incredible wisdom. His reign was marked by great wealth and influence throughout the world. His greatest achievement was the construction of a magnificent temple for the Lord.

After Solomon died, the nation split into two kingdoms: the northern kingdom of Israel and the southern kingdom of Judah, which was still ruled by David's descendants. These two kingdoms—especially the northern kingdom—were marked by great sin and idolatry throughout the remainder of their history. Occasionally the southern kingdom would experience revival (usually initiated by the king) and would return to the worship of the Lord, but the northern kingdom appears to have been much more corrupt. Their first king even formally instituted the worship of idols in the towns of Dan and Bethel.

Eventually the sins of both kingdoms caught up with them. The northern kingdom was captured by the Assyrians in 722 B.C., and the people were exiled. The southern kingdom held on until around 586 B.C., when they were captured by the Babylonians under Nebuchadnezzar. The Babylonians exiled many people to Babylon, and the Temple was destroyed.

Several decades later, the Persians conquered the Babylonians and issued a decree that all exiles could return to their native lands. So many Israelites (who were beginning to be called Jews) returned to their homeland. Others, however, continued to live in Babylon. The Jews who returned soon rebuilt the Temple, and worship was restored. About sixty years later, a man named Ezra returned to Judah along with many other exiles, and he initiated a time of repentance and renewed study of the Scriptures. Another man, Nehemiah, also returned and rebuilt the walls around Jerusalem.

The Authors of the Old Testament

In modern times books have authors' names on the front cover or on the title page. In ancient times the name of the author was not always on the book. This is especially true for the books of the Bible, which are all ancient. Only a few books of the Bible include the author's name. Consequently, we have to rely on other sources that tell us about who wrote a particular book or books of the Bible.

Traditionally, Moses has been ascribed authorship of the books of the Law, which consists of the first five books of the Old Testament. Several Old Testament writers considered him to be the writer (2 Kings 14:6; Ezra 3:2; Daniel 9:11), as did Jesus (Luke 24:44) and Paul (1 Corinthians 9:9). These books are also called the Pentateuch (literally, "five in a case"—referring to five scrolls in a case). They provided the Israelites with instructions and principles for personal, social, and spiritual life. In short, they contain the essence of Judaism.

Next in the Christian arrangement come the historical books. Traditionally, Joshua is thought to be the author of the book that bears his name, although the book itself does not say this. Judges is thought to have been written by Samuel on the basis that he was the last of the judges. It is doubtful that he wrote 1 and 2 Samuel, however, since his death is recorded in 1 Samuel. The "Samuel" who wrote the books 1 and 2 Samuel is most likely Samuel the Seer (or "the Prophet"), whose writing is mentioned in 1 Chronicles 29:29. We do not know who wrote Ruth (a story about a Moabite woman during the period of the judges), Esther (a story about a Jewish heroine during the Persian era), or 1 and 2 Kings (a record of the various kings of Israel and Judah from the time of Solomon to the Exile). The rest of the historical writings (1 and 2 Chronicles, Ezra, and Nehemiah) were probably written by Ezra, who is described as a knowledgeable and well-trained scribe.

As for the poetic books, it is thought that Job was written by Job, but we do not know this with certainty, nor do we know when this book was written. The Book of Psalms was composed by a number of individuals, including Asaph, David, and the descendants of Korah, whose names are mentioned in the titles to some psalms. Psalms functioned very much like Israel's hymnbook, with different psalms addressing different occasions and situations. Some of the psalms were written from the perspective of a single individual, and these could be joyful or sorrowful, meditative or exhuberant. Others were written as songs for the entire community to sing to the Lord, and often they celebrated national victories or praised the king. Most of the book of Proverbs probably came from Solomon. A few were authored by Agur and Lemuel. Song of Songs is said to be Solomon's (1:1). Solomon is usually also credited with Ecclesiastes, but scholars are uncertain about this.

The authorship of the prophets is often more certain because the prophet's name is identified in the book—usually in the first verse. The prophetic books are a record of God's oracles to his people concerning past, present, and future events. Most of them were written during the period of the divided kingdom, and they often address issues such as sin and wickedness. The books of Haggai, Zechariah, and Malachi were written after the people returned from exile.

Over time, the books of the Old Testament were collected into three major sections: the Law, the Prophets, and the Writings. In the New Testament, when Jesus spoke to his disciples about the Old Testament, he referred to this same threefold division as he said, "When I was with you before, I told you that everything written about me by Moses and the prophets and in the Psalms [which are part of the Writings] must all come true" (Luke 24:44).

The section of the Hebrew Bible called the Prophets comprises a very large segment of writings. The Prophets include the four historical books of Joshua, Judges, 1 and 2 Samuel (originally written as a single book), and 1 and 2 Kings (also originally written as a single book). The Prophets also include the books of the three major prophets (Isaiah, Jeremiah, and Ezekiel) and the books of the twelve minor prophets (Hosea, Joel, Amos, Obadiah, Jonah, Micah, Nahum, Habbakuk, Zephaniah, Haggai, Zechariah, and Malachi).

In the Hebrew Bible the last section is entitled the Writings and contains two kinds of literature. The first kind includes Psalms, Proverbs, Job, Song of Songs, Lamentations, and Ecclesiastes. Most of these books are poetic in form and thought, and many of them, especially Proverbs and Ecclesiastes, make "wisdom" a central theme. Ruth is included among these books as a preface to Psalms, since it ends with the genealogy of the psalmist David. The second kind of literature in the Writings includes historical books, specifically Esther, Daniel, Ezra-Nehemiah (regarded as a single book in the Hebrew Bible), and 1 and 2 Chronicles (originally written as a single book).

The grouping and ordering of the books in the Hebrew

Bible is different from the way Christians normally see them
in their Bibles today. This is because the Christian Bible
adopted the order found in the Septuagint, a Greek translation
of the Hebrew Bible. The Septuagint was produced in the
third century B.C. by Jewish scribes versed in Hebrew and
Greek. This translation became very popular among Jews in
the first two centuries before Christ because many Jews in
those days did not understand Hebrew. Their ancestors had
left the land of Israel centuries before, and generation after
generation gradually lost the ability to read the Scriptures in
Hebrew. Many of the Jews in Jesus' day used the Septuagint
as their Bible. Quite naturally, the early Christians also used
the Septuagint in their meetings and for personal reading,
and many of the New Testament apostles quoted it when they
wrote the Gospels and Epistles in Greek.

The following is a list of the probable authors of the Old
Testament books, which have been arranged according to the
Christian Bible.

PROBABLE AUTHORS OF THE
OLD TESTAMENT BOOKS

Law (or Pentateuch)
Genesis . . . . *Moses*
Exodus. . . . . *Moses*
Leviticus . . . . *Moses*
Numbers . . . . *Moses*
Deuteronomy. . . . . *Moses*

History
Joshua . . . . *Joshua*
Judges . . . . *Samuel (?)*
Ruth. *Unknown*
1 and 2 Samuel . . . . *Samuel the Seer?*
1 and 2 Kings . . . . *Unknown*

1 and 2 Chronicles. . . . . *Ezra*
Ezra . . . . *Ezra*
Nehemiah . . . . *Ezra*
Esther . . . . *Unknown*

Wisdom and Poetry
Job. . . . . *Job (?)*
Psalms . . . . *Asaph, David, and others*
Proverbs . . . . *Solomon, Agur, Lemuel*
Ecclesiastes . . . . *Solomon (?)*
Song of Songs . . . . *Solomon (?)*

Major Prophets
Isaiah. . . . . *Isaiah*
Jeremiah . . . . *Jeremiah*
Lamentations. . . . . *Jeremiah*
Ezekiel. . . . . *Ezekiel*
Daniel . . . . *Daniel*

Minor Prophets
Hosea. . . . . *Hosea*
Joel . . . . *Joel*
Amos. . . . . *Amos*
Obadiah. . . . . *Obadiah*
Jonah . . . . *Jonah (?)*
Micah . . . . *Micah*
Nahum. . . . . *Nahum*
Habbakuk . . . . *Habbakuk*
Zephaniah . . . . *Zephaniah*
Haggai. . . . . *Haggai*
Zechariah. . . . . *Zechariah*
Malachi . . . . *Malachi*

The following chart summarizes the arrangement of the books in the Hebrew Bible:

THE HEBREW BIBLE

The Law	The Prophets	The Writings
Genesis	Joshua	Psalms
Exodus	Judges	Proverbs
Leviticus	1 and 2 Samuel	Job
Numbers	1 and 2 Kings	Song of Songs
Deuteronomy		Ruth
	Isaiah	Lamentations
	Jeremiah	Ecclesiastes
	Ezekiel	Esther
		Daniel
	Hosea	Ezra-Nehemiah
	Joel	1 and 2 Chronicles
	Amos	
	Obadiah	
	Jonah	
	Micah	
	Nahum	
	Habbakuk	
	Zephaniah	
	Haggai	
	Zechariah	
	Malachi	

THE OLD TESTAMENT CANON

The canon of Scripture designates those books in the Hebrew and Christian Bibles that are considered Scripture and therefore authoritative in matters of faith and doctrine. The term *canon* comes from the Greek word *kanon,* which means "a rule," or "a measuring rod." Hence, the canon is a list to which other books are compared and by which they are measured. After the fourth century A.D., most Christian churches considered sixty-six books to be Scripture; thirty-nine of these were the Old Testament, and twenty-seven were the New Testament.

The criteria for selecting the books in the Hebrew canon (the

Old Testament) are not precisely known, but no doubt one criterion was their worth in the ongoing life and worship of God's people. Actually, the phrase "Old Testament" never appears in Jewish literature. Jews prefer to call their thirty-nine books of Scripture the TANAK—an acronym formed from the first letters of the words *Torah* (Law), *Nevi'im* (Prophets), and *Kethuvim* (Writings).

Jewish religion existed for a millennium, from Moses to Malachi (i.e., about 1400–400 B.C.), without a closed canon—an exclusive list of authoritative books. Never in their ancient history did the people of the Old Testament have the entire thirty-nine books of the Old Testament. As to when their canon was closed is not known. It seems that the canon was generally agreed upon by the time of Jesus. Official recognition of the final Hebrew canon seems to have been made at Jammia in A.D. 90 by a group of Jewish rabbis. The first actual list of the thirty-nine books of the Old Testament was produced by Melito of Sardis around A.D. 170. That list included no books written after the time of Malachi.

The thirty-nine books of the modern Old Testament were originally divided into only twenty-four. This arrangement included five books of the Law, eight books of Prophets, and eleven books of Writings. The Law contained the Pentateuch in our familiar order, Genesis to Deuteronomy. The eight Prophets were Joshua, Judges, Samuel (1 and 2), Kings (1 and 2), Isaiah, Jeremiah, and Ezekiel; the Minor Prophets (twelve) were considered the eighth book and arranged in the same order as were in our English Bibles. The eleven books of Writings contained three of poetry (Psalms, Proverbs, Job); five of Rolls (Songs, Ruth, Lamentations, Ecclesiastes, Esther), which were read at the important religious festivals and arranged in the chronological order of their observance; and three historical books (Daniel, Ezra-Nehemiah, 1 and 2 Chronicles).

THE LANGUAGES OF THE OLD TESTAMENT: HEBREW AND ARAMAIC

Most of the Old Testament was written in Hebrew. Hebrew was one of several Canaanite dialects, which included also Phoenician, Ugaritic, and Moabite. Such dialects were already present in the land of Canaan before its conquest by the Israelites.

The Hebrew alphabet consists of twenty-two consonants; signs for vowels were devised and added late in the language's history. The exact origin of the alphabet is unknown. The oldest examples of a Canaanite alphabet were preserved in the Ugaritic cuneiform alphabet of the fourteenth century B.C. The old style of writing the letters is called the Phoenician or paleo-Hebrew script. The script used in modern Hebrew Bibles (Aramaic or square script) came into common use after Israel's exile into Babylon (sixth century B.C.). The older style was still used sporadically in the early Christian era on coins and for writing the tetragrammaton (the four-letter name for God, YHWH). Hebrew has always been written right to left.

A few sections of the Old Testament were written in Aramaic, a sister language of Hebrew: Daniel 2:4–7:28 and Ezra 4:8–6:18; 7:12–26. Aramaic phrases and expressions also appear in Genesis 31:47, Jeremiah 10:11, and the New Testament. Aramaic has one of the longest living histories of any language known. It was used during the Bible's patriarchal period and is still spoken by some people today. The origin of Aramaic is unknown, but it seems to have been closely related to Amorite and possibly to other ancient northwest Semitic dialects barely known to scholars. By the eighth century B.C., King Hezekiah's representatives requested the spokesmen of the Assyrian king Sennacherib to "please speak to us in Aramaic, for we understand it well. Don't speak in Hebrew, for the people on the wall will hear" (2 Kings 18:26). By the Persian period, Aramaic had become the language of international trade. During their captivity the Jews probably adopted Aramaic for convenience—certainly in commerce—while Hebrew became confined to the learned and to religious leaders. This is evidenced by Nehemiah's complaint that children from mixed marriages were unable to speak Hebrew (Nehemiah 13:24). The Jews seem to have continued using Aramaic widely during the Persian, Greek, and Roman periods. In fact, it was probably the ethnic language of Jesus. Eventually, the Hebrew Scriptures were translated into Aramaic paraphrases, called Targums, some of which have been found among the Dead Sea Scrolls (see "How We Got the Old Testament").

OLD TESTAMENT MANUSCRIPTS

Not one of the original writings (called the "autographs") of any book in the Old Testament still exists today. Fortunately, Jewish scribes throughout the ages have made copies of God's Word. Jewish scribes took meticulous care in producing copies of the Scripture because they regarded the text as being God-given and God-inspired down to the very letter. Jesus had the same regard for the Old Testament text; on several occasions he affirmed the immutability of every word of the text (Matthew 5:17-18; John 10:34-35).

In ancient times scribes used quills, ink, and leather scrolls to make copies of individual books of the Bible. Some of the scrolls, made of several treated animal hides stitched together, could be as long as thirty-five to forty feet when unrolled. As scrolls wore out or the need arose for copies in other synagogues, Jewish scribes would make additional copies—and they did so with painstaking care. It is known that scribes would count the number of letters on the new copy and compare it with the exemplar in an attempt to find even one letter difference between the two. If the copy was in error, it would be corrected or destroyed. This practice continued generation after generation, century after century.

Masoretic Manuscripts
Beginning in the sixth century and into the tenth century A.D., certain European Jewish scribes, the Masoretes, continued to carefully preserve the Old Testament text as they transmitted it from copy to copy. The Hebrew word *masorah* means "that which is transmitted," or "that which is handed down"; hence, the name Masoretes. Most scholars think the Masoretes were simply carrying on a tradition that began a century before Christ. Several of the manuscripts the European Masoretes produced still exist. Some of the more important Masoretic manuscripts are as follows:

> *The Cairo Codex of the Prophets*
> Dated A.D. 895, it contains the Prophets.

> *The British Museum Codex Oriental 4445*
> Dated in the ninth or tenth century, it contains a large portion of the Pentateuch.

> *The Leningrad Codex of the Prophets*
> Dated A.D. 916, it contains the Major Prophets.

> *The Leningrad Codex*
> Dated A.D. 1008–1009, it is the earliest codex to contain the complete Old Testament text.

> *The Aleppo Codex*
> Dated A.D. 900–925, this codex originally had the entire Old Testament text, but a quarter of its text is missing.

Dead Sea Scroll Manuscripts
Until the twentieth century, the Masoretic manuscripts were the oldest copies of the Old Testament in existence. A few other

earlier manuscripts were discovered around the turn of the twentieth century. The first such discovery was the Cairo Geniza Fragments. As many as 200,000 fragments, including biblical texts in Hebrew and Aramaic (dated to the fifth century A.D.), were found in the genizah (a storage room) of an old synagogue in Cairo, Egypt. The second such discovery was the Nash Papyrus, acquired in Egypt by W. L. Nash in 1902. This manuscript contains a damaged copy of the Ten Commandments (Exodus 20:2-17) and part of Deuteronomy 5:6-21; 6:4-8. It has been dated between 150 B.C. and A.D. 68.

Then in 1947 and 1948, the year Israel regained its national independence, there was a phenomenal discovery. A Bedouin shepherd boy found scrolls in a cave west of the Dead Sea. When scholars compared the style of handwriting on the scrolls with a photograph of the Nash Papyrus, they concluded that the newly found manuscripts, known as the Dead Sea Scrolls, belonged to the same period. Thus, the Dead Sea Scrolls, dated between 100 B.C. and A.D. 100, are a thousand years earlier than any of the Masoretic manuscripts.

The Dead Sea Scrolls contain significant portions of the Old Testament. Every book except Esther is represented. The largest portions come from the Pentateuch (especially Deuteronomy—twenty-five manuscripts), the Major Prophets (especially Isaiah—eighteen manuscripts), and Psalms (twenty-seven manuscripts). The Dead Sea Scrolls also have portions of the Septuagint, the Targums, some apocryphal fragments, and a commentary on Habakkuk. The scribes who made these scrolls were members of a community of ascetic Jews who lived in Qumran from the third century B.C. to the first century A.D.

Even though the Dead Sea Scrolls are nearly a thousand years older than the Masoretic manuscripts, there are not as many significant differences between the two groups of manuscripts as one would expect. Normally, a thousand years of copying would have generated thousands of differences in wording. But this is not the case with the Dead Sea Scrolls and the Masoretic manuscripts. This shows that Jewish scribes for over a millennium copied one form of the text with extreme accuracy.

Some of the more noteworthy Dead Sea Scroll manuscripts are listed below. (The first number signifies the cave number; *Q* indicates Qumran; the abbreviation for the biblical book follows, often followed by a superscipt letter for successive manuscripts containing the same book.)

1QIsa^a

This is the first Dead Sea Scroll to receive widespread attention. It is dated to about 100 B.C. The text, which includes most of Isaiah, appears to be an early form of the Masoretic Text with some significant differences.

1QIsa^b

The text, which includes most of Isaiah, also appears to be an early form of the Masoretic Text. It is dated between 25 B.C. and A.D. 50.

2QJer

This manuscript is dated between 25 B.C. and A.D. 50 and has portions of chapters 42–49. It has some readings that follow the Septuagint, but it follows the order of chapters found in early forms of the Masoretic Text. For the book of Jeremiah, the Septuagint and Masoretic Text are quite different: The Septuagint is one-eighth shorter and has a different arrangement of chapters.

4QPaleoExod^m

This manuscript, containing most of Exodus, is dated quite early: 200–175 B.C. As such, it has provided scholars with some interesting insights into the early history of the textual transmission of Exodus and the rest of the Pentateuch.

4QNum*b*

This manuscript, dated between 30 B.C. and A.D. 20, contains most of the book of Numbers. This book of the Old Testament existed in three distinguishable textual traditions: the Masoretic Text, the Samaritan Pentateuch, and the Septuagint. This manuscript, 4QNum*b*, shows similarities with the Samaritan Pentateuch and the Septuagint, while having its own unique readings.

4QSam*a*

This manuscript, containing about a tenth of 1 and 2 Samuel, is dated to about 50–25 B.C. Its text shows some similarities with the Septuagint and has several readings that are believed by many to be closer to the original text than those found in the Masoretic Text.

4QJer*a*

This manuscript, containing portions of Jeremiah 7–22, dates to about 200 B.C. It generally concurs with the Masoretic Text.

4QJer*b*

This manuscript, dated to about 150–125 B.C., follows the arrangement of the Septuagint as well as its brevity. The significance of this is that two different texts of Jeremiah were used in the pre-Christian era—one that was an early form of the Masoretic Text (as with 4QJer*a*) and one that was like the Septuagint.

11QPs*a*

This manuscript, dated to about A.D. 25–50, preserves the text of many psalms. However, these psalms are not in the traditional sequence found in the Hebrew Bible. Furthermore, the manuscript has several other psalms, some of which were known from other ancient versions and others that were unknown until they surfaced in this manuscript.

MODERN EDITIONS OF THE HEBREW OLD TESTAMENT

To this day almost all Bible scholars still use the Masoretic Text of the Hebrew Bible as the authoritative, standard text. At the same time, they make use of the findings of the Dead Sea Scrolls, as well as two other important sources: the Septuagint (see discussion in chapter 4) and the Samaritan Pentateuch (i.e., the Pentateuch as transcribed and edited by the Samaritans). The Masoretic Text with up-to-date textual notes is published in an edition called *Biblia Hebraica Stuttgartensia* (1967, 1977).

How We Got the New Testament

Whereas the Old Testament was written over hundreds of years, the New Testament was completed within the span of fifty years, during the second half of the first century A.D. In various ways all of the books of the New Testament center upon one person—Jesus Christ. Some of the books tell of Jesus' life and ministry; these are called Gospels. Another, the book of Acts, tells of the birth and spread of the church, which is made up of those who believe in Jesus Christ and who meet together to worship and celebrate his death and resurrection. Still other books were written as letters, or epistles, to various people and churches. These epistles give instructions regarding matters of both theology and Christian living. The book of Revelation, which seems to be a cross between an epistle and a prophetic vision, appropriately concludes the New Testament (and the Bible) with a message about the future and the end of time, when Jesus Christ will reign over the whole earth.

A BRIEF HISTORY

In order to understand where the books of the New Testament came from, we must first learn about the important people and events that shaped these books.

The Life and Ministry of Jesus Christ

As we mentioned earlier, all of the New Testament books center upon the person and ministry of Jesus Christ. Jesus is the unique Son of God and the head of the church. His life and ministry made the old covenant, which is described in the Old Testament, obsolete and established the New Covenant with all believers, giving all people a way to come to God through faith in his Son.

Jesus' "beginnings" actually go back before his birth to Mary. The apostle John describes Jesus as "the Word," who has existed from the very beginning of time (John 1:1). John adds that Jesus was with God and that he *was* God. Yet John and the other New Testament writers also describe Jesus as the Son of God (John 1:14).

Regarding Jesus' earthly life, he was born during the reign of Herod the Great, around 5 B.C. (The B.C./A.D. dating system was developed hundreds of years after Jesus' birth, and it was probably off a few years.) At this time the land of Israel had undergone many changes since the last book of the Old Testament (Malachi) was written. The Persians, who ruled over the Jews during Malachi's time, were conquered by Alexander the Great, whose kingdom was quickly divided among four generals. Two of these generals were Seleucus, who ruled over modern-day Syria, and Ptolemy, who ruled over Egypt. The land of Israel, or "Palestine" as it came to be called, was sandwiched between these two kingdoms, and as a result it was the battleground for many disputes between the two kingdoms.

Eventually, Palestine came under the firm control of the Seleucids, who began to oppress the Jews, forcing them to abandon their religious distinctions and conform to Greek customs. This caused a great uprising, led by a family known as the Maccabees. In time, this family allowed the Jews to gain independence once again. Eventually, however, the Romans took over Palestine, and they later placed the region under the rule of Herod the Great, an Idumean, not a Jew.

We should also note a couple of social developments that occurred during this period between the two testaments of the Bible. First, the Jews began to establish synagogues, local places where they could gather to learn about and observe the Law of Moses and other books of the Old Testament. Second, there arose several politico-religious parties within Palestine. These included the Pharisees (who strictly adhered to the Law and the teachings of their rabbis), the Sadducees (mostly priests who denied many of the beliefs held by the Pharisees, such as the resurrection of the dead), the Essenes (who were even stricter than the Pharisees in their adherence to the Law), and various anti-Roman parties, such as the Zealots. All these groups would have touched Jesus' life in some way or another as he lived and ministered in Palestine.

As was mentioned earlier, it was near the end of Herod the Great's reign that Jesus was born. The Gospels tell us that Jesus was conceived by the Holy Spirit, who came upon a virgin named Mary. Jesus' earthly, adoptive father was a carpenter named Joseph, a descendant of King David. Jesus was born in Bethlehem and grew up in the small town of Nazareth in Galilee, a northern territory of Palestine. Not much else is known of Jesus' early life, except that he grew in wisdom and possessed great knowledge of spiritual matters by the age of twelve (Luke 2:41-52).

When Jesus reached the age of thirty, he began his formal ministry period. This was initiated with his baptism by his cousin, John the Baptist, who had already established a widespread ministry of his own. Early in his ministry, Jesus began preaching essentially the same message that John the Baptist had preached: "The Kingdom of God is near! Turn from your sins and believe this Good News!" (Mark 1:15).

For most of his early ministry, Jesus traveled throughout the region surrounding the Sea of Galilee. In his hometown of Nazareth, Jesus made his mission clear: "The Spirit of the Lord is upon me, for he has appointed me to preach Good News to the poor. He has sent me to proclaim that captives will be released, that the blind will see, that the downtrodden will be freed from their oppressors, and that the time of the Lord's favor has come" (Luke 4:18-19). This statement, taken from the Old Testament (Isaiah 61:1-2), made it clear that Jesus was God's anointed (Greek *christos*)—that is, Jesus was the long-awaited Messiah written about by the Old Testament writers. Jesus then began his travels, healing the sick and casting out demons. He also began teaching about God and his Kingdom, often through the form of stories, or parables. These teachings often clashed with those of the Pharisees and other leaders of his day. Along the way Jesus selected twelve disciples as his special followers. These men lived and traveled with Jesus, listening to his teachings and witnessing his miracles. In time, they would be instrumental in the establishment of the Christian church.

After three years of ministry, Jesus made a final trip to Jerusalem. Throughout his ministry he had told his disciples that he would eventually suffer and die in Jerusalem at the hands of his enemies. This is exactly what happened. On the Sunday before Passover, Jesus entered Jerusalem triumphantly, with all the people bowing down before him and shouting, "Bless the one who comes in the name of the Lord!" (Mark 11:9). Just a few days later, however, Jesus was arrested by the Temple guard, put on trial, and executed as a criminal by the Roman governor Pontius Pilate. All this, however, was in fulfillment of the Old Testament prophecies of the Messiah's ministry (see especially Isaiah 53:1-12).

But the story does not stop there. On the third day after his death, Jesus arose from the dead! He first appeared to some women disciples and then later to all the disciples. For forty days

he remained on earth, proving to his disciples that he was truly
alive and teaching them further about the Kingdom of God.
Finally, Jesus was taken up into heaven, where he was seated
at the right hand of God the Father.

The Birth and Spread of the Church

About a week after Jesus ascended to heaven, the disciples (who
were now called apostles, meaning "sent ones") were gathered
together in a room in Jerusalem. Suddenly, everyone in the room
was filled with the Holy Spirit, and all of them began speaking in
different languages. This took place during the festival of Pente-
cost, when Jews from all over the world were visiting Jerusalem.
After a while the apostle Peter stepped forward and began preaching about Jesus, declaring him to be the Messiah, who was cruci-
fied and raised to life again. Thousands of people responded to
his message and repented of their sins. They were baptized in the
name of Jesus Christ and committed themselves to meet together
to pray, listen to the apostles' teaching, and celebrate the Lord's
Supper. The Lord's Supper had been established by Jesus as a way
for his followers to remember him. It involved partaking of bread,
representing the Lord's broken body, and drinking wine, representing the Lord's shed blood. This coming of the Holy Spirit and
gathering of believers marked the birth of the church.

Soon after this, Peter and the apostles began taking the message of Jesus throughout the world, despite many persecutions.
One of their persecutors was a zealous Jew named Saul, who
had been given special orders to hunt down and arrest Christians.
One day as Saul was traveling to Damascus, the Lord Jesus
appeared to him and spoke to him, and Saul became a new fol-
lower of Jesus. Over time, the church, which was initially leery
of this new persecutor-turned-follower, came to trust that Saul's
conversion was genuine. Saul, who soon began using his Latin
name, Paul, exclusively, became a great leader and teacher in the

church, and he was considered one of the apostles as well. Throughout his lifetime he made three trips throughout Asia Minor and Greece, planting and strengthening churches along the way. Paul was a key figure in the establishment of the gospel (the "Good News" about Jesus) among the Gentiles, or non-Jews. Many of the books of the New Testament are actually letters, or epistles, written by Paul to the churches.

Around A.D. 59, Paul returned to Jerusalem from his third missionary journey. Soon after his arrival, Paul was attacked at the Temple by a Jewish mob who was angry at him for his role in converting many—including Gentiles—to Jesus Christ. A Roman officer arrested Paul, and just before Paul was about to be flogged, he appealed to his right as a Roman citizen to appear before Caesar. So he was eventually sent to Rome, where he lived under house arrest for a couple of years before being released. A few years later, Paul was arrested again, and it is believed that he was martyred in Rome by Nero.

The other apostles continued their ministries, traveling throughout the known world spreading the Good News about Jesus. It appears that the apostle Peter eventually came to live in Rome, and the apostle John lived in Ephesus until he was exiled to the island of Patmos, where he recorded the book of Revelation and then died. John's death marked the end of the apostolic age, that is, the era when the church was under the direct leadership of living apostles.

THE AUTHORS OF THE NEW TESTAMENT

Though stories of the life and teachings of Jesus (called "Gospels") come first in the New Testament, it was actually the Epistles that were the first to be written.

The Epistles were written by Paul and other apostles to various churches and individuals in order to instruct them in the faith and give practical guidance. Some scholars have drawn a distinction between a letter and an epistle. By their definition, a letter is a direct personal correspondence between two people, not intended to be read by others. An epistle, on the other hand, is a stylized literary form that gives the impression of being personally directed to one or more individuals but whose real intent is to address a much wider audience. This distinction, however, has been challenged by other scholars in recent years in light of many new discoveries of personal and offical letters from the period of the early church.

Paul's Letters

Paul's letters to the Galatians, Thessalonians, Colossians, Philippians, and Corinthians were all written to specific churches, so they give a great deal of specific advice to the congregations for whom they were written. There is also general instruction and theology interspersed among the practical instruction. Two of Paul's other epistles, Romans and Ephesians, were more general and theological in nature. Ephesians is even thought to have been written as an encyclical, a letter to be passed among several churches. Romans is Paul's great treatise on Christianity, and Ephesians is Paul's masterpiece about the church.

Paul's letters to Timothy, Titus, and Philemon were written to specific individuals. In his letters to Timothy and Titus, Paul instructs these young associates in how to lead their churches well and exhorts them to do so. For this reason, these letters are often referred to as the Pastoral Epistles. Paul's letter to Philemon was probably sent along with his letter to the Colossians, and it addresses a personal matter about one of Philemon's runaway slaves who had since become Paul's assistant.

General Epistles

At the end of the New Testament there are several letters called General Epistles. They are called "general" because most of them are addressed to the church at large.

The first of these General Epistles is Hebrews. Some have thought this anonymous letter was written by Paul, but this is now thought to be unlikely. Many scholars think it was written by Apollos, an early Christian teacher from Alexandria, who was a gifted speaker. This letter warns Jewish Christians against falling away from the faith and returning to Judaism.

The apostle Peter wrote two letters as well. His first letter, written with the help of an associate named Silas, appears to have been an encyclical to churches in Asia Minor, and his second one may have been as well. The first letter was written to encourage the believers who were suffering persecution for their faith. The second letter gives warnings against falling away from the faith.

The apostle John wrote three epistles. They are also a mix of general and specific instruction in the faith.

One of the earliest epistles to be written was probably James's letter to all believers scattered throughout the Roman Empire. James was an apostle and the half brother of Jesus, and he led the Jerusalem church. It is not surprising, then, that this letter has a distinct Jewish feel to its style and wording. This practical letter calls believers to live in a truly Christian manner.

Jude, another apostle and half brother of Jesus, wrote one epistle of general instruction and warning against falling away.

The Gospels

When the church was first established, there were many—including the twelve apostles—who had been with Jesus throughout his ministry and who could attest to what he taught and did. But as the church began to grow and spread, it was more difficult for these people to communicate Jesus' words to all who needed to hear them. Also, as time went on, the apostles began to die off, leaving fewer and fewer apostles to carry out this task. This created a demand for the apostles' teachings about Jesus' life and sayings to be recorded on paper so that many churches could learn and follow them without requiring an apostle to be with them. These accounts, called Gospels (meaning "Good News"), would also ensure that the apostles' message would not be lost after they had all died.

Exactly when were the apostles' messages about Jesus put into writing? It is possible that someone like Matthew could have taken notes on Jesus' speeches, then later used these notes or memoranda to compose a Gospel. This much is certain: By the time Luke began to do research for his Gospel (which was probably in the early 60s, if not earlier), Gospels (plural) about Jesus already existed in written form. We can gather this from reading Luke's preface (1:1-4). According to Luke, many written accounts of Jesus' ministry had been circulating prior to the time he composed his Gospel. Luke was probably referring to Mark and Matthew—or maybe even John, as well as some unknown works. Evidently, the early believers would have known these works.

Luke also mentioned that he wrote his Gospel account to affirm what Theophilus had already been taught. The Greek expression in 1:4 is very revealing. In an expanded rendering, it could be translated, "that you might know the certainty of the words you have been taught by word of mouth." Theophilus, typical of most Christians in that era, had received the sayings of Jesus by oral recitation. But Luke felt that Theophilus needed a written affirmation of what he had been taught orally. It is important to note that Luke didn't say his written account would change the oral account in any way. Rather, the written would affirm or substantiate the oral. As such, the written Gospel became an accurate extension and continuation of the oral. Mark, tradition tells us, compiled a Gospel based on Peter's oral messages about Jesus' ministry. And many scholars believe that John first preached many of the chapters he later weaved into his Gospel narrative. Thus, the Gospel was first published in oral form, then in written form.

In none of the Gospels does the author identify himself by name. However, early and widespread tradition indicates who the authors were. The author of the Gospel placed at the beginning of the New Testament was Matthew, one of Jesus' twelve apostles, and he probably finished his work around A.D. 70. The second Gospel, probably the first to be written (about A.D. 50), was composed by John Mark on the basis of Peter's preaching and recollections. We know that the author of the third Gospel is Luke, who also wrote the book of Acts (detailing the birth and growth of the early church) as a sequel to his Gospel (which was written about A.D. 60). Luke tells his readers that he based his written Gospel on the accounts given to him by Jesus' eyewitnesses (see Luke 1:1-4). The fourth Gospel was written by Jesus' "beloved disciple," John, around A.D. 85–90.

Apparently, both Matthew and Luke used Mark's Gospel when they wrote their own, since both Matthew and Luke contain much of the same material as Mark.

Revelation

Probably the last New Testament book to be written was Revelation, which differs from the other New Testament writings in literary genre and subject matter. It is a combination of both epistle and prophecy, and it contains both warning and consolation—announcements of future judgment and blessing communicated by means of symbols and visions. This writing falls under the category of apocalyptic, coming from the Greek word *apokalupsis* (meaning "unveiling" or "revealing"). It was written by the apostle John while he was exiled to the island of Patmos. The first section contains a letter to seven churches in Asia Minor, and the second part recounts his grand vision foretelling future events.

To the best of our knowledge, then, the authors of the New Testament books are as follows:

PROBABLE AUTHORS OF THE
NEW TESTAMENT BOOKS

Gospels and Acts

Matthew .... Matthew (the apostle)

Mark .... Mark (with Peter)

Luke .... Luke (Paul's coworker)

John..................... John (the apostle)

Acts..................... Luke (Paul's coworker)

Paul's Epistles

Romans

1 Corinthians

2 Corinthians

Galatians

Ephesians

Philippians

Colossians

1 Thessalonians

2 Thessalonians

1 Timothy

2 Timothy

Titus

Philemon

General Epistles and Revelation

Hebrews .... Anonymous (Apollos'?)

James.................... James (Jesus' half brother)

1 Peter.................. Peter (with Silvanus)

2 Peter.................. Peter

1 John .... John (the apostle)

2 John .... John (the apostle)

3 John .... John (the apostle)

Jude..................... Jude (Jesus' half brother)

Revelation............... John (the apostle)

THE NEW TESTAMENT CANON

In the first century, Christians treated the Old Testament (as it was later called) as Scripture. They read the Old Testament and spoke from it in their meetings (see Ephesians 5:19; Colossians 3:16; 2 Timothy 3:14-17). They also had the testimony and teachings of the apostles who were still living. Essentially, the apostles were those who had been Jesus' disciples while he lived on earth. These men were given authority over the teachings of the church once Christ returned to heaven. The apostles taught them the gospel of Jesus the Messiah and passed on to them the teachings of Jesus. But as the apostles grew older and some of them died, Christians came to depend more and more on what the apostles had *written.* At the same time, they began to recognize the apostles' writings as being on a par with the Old Testament writings. This was the beginning of the formation of the New Testament canon.

As we mentioned regarding the Old Testament, the word *canon* comes from the Greek word *kanon,* meaning "a rule" or "a measuring rod." A canon, therefore, indicates a standard of measurement. Before a book could be included in the New Testament canon, it had to measure up to this standard: (1) it had to be authored by an apostle, an associate of an apostle, or a relative of Jesus (i.e., James and Jude); (2) it had to contain divinely inspired truths that could be taught as Christian doctrine; and (3) it had to be regarded by successive generations of Christians as edifying, enlightening, and inspiring. The formation of the New Testament canon was a process, rather than an event, that took several hundred years to reach finality in all parts of the Roman Empire.

After the various books of the New Testament were written and began to circulate among the churches, Christians collected certain books into single volumes. In the first century, each of the four Gospels was treated as an individual book about Jesus' life and ministry. By the end of the first century, many churches had collected Paul's epistles into one volume. Beginning in the late second century, Christians began to collect the four Gospels into one volume. This collection became known as "The Gospel: According to Matthew, According to Mark, According to Luke, According to John." Later, in the second and third centuries, other Christians began to combine Acts with the General Epistles in one volume.

By the second century, several of the books of the New Testament were considered to be divinely inspired Scripture: the four Gospels, Acts, Paul's epistles, 1 Peter, and 1 John. Other books took longer to gain full recognition: Hebrews (because the author was unknown), James (because it was thought to have doctrinal differences with Paul's theology on salvation), 2 Peter and Jude (over the question of authorship), 2 and 3 John (because they were not well known), and Revelation (because its message and authorship were debated). By the middle of the fourth century, however, most issues had been resolved, and these books were also accepted by the church as divinely inspired and worthy of inclusion in the New Testament canon.

Irenaeus (a disciple of Polycarp, who was himself a disciple of the apostle John) had affirmed the canonicity of the fourfold Gospel in the second century. This fourfold Gospel continued to be confirmed by later Christian scholars, such as Hippolytus, Novatian, Tertullian, Cyprian, Clement of Alexandria, Origen, and Dionysius. These writers also affirmed the canonical status of most of the other books of the New Testament, while recording doubts about such books as 2 Peter, Jude, 2 and 3 John, and Revelation. In the beginning of the fourth century, the well-known church historian Eusebius sought to establish the New Testament canon as consisting of those books which we now regard as Scripture today. This twenty-seven-book canon was established once and for all by Athanasius of Alexandria in the fourth century. In his Festal Letter for Easter (A.D. 367), Athanasius listed the twenty-seven books of the New Testament and admonished his readers, "Let no one add to these; let nothing be taken away." This provides the earliest extant document which specifies the twenty-seven books without qualification. At the close of the century, the Council of Carthage (A.D. 397) decreed that "aside from the canonical Scriptures nothing is to be read in church under the Name of Divine Scriptures." The council also listed the twenty-seven books of the New Testament as we have them today.

THE LANGUAGE OF THE NEW TESTAMENT: GREEK

During its classical period, Greek was the language of one of the world's greatest cultures. The Greek language reflected artistry in its philosophical dialogues, its poetry, and its stately speeches. Classical Greek elaborately developed many forms from a few word roots. Its complex rules of grammar allowed intricate word arrangements to express fine nuances of meaning.

At the close of the classical Greek era, the conquests of Alexander the Great encouraged the spread of Greek language and culture. Regional dialects were largely replaced by Hellenistic or *Koine* (common) Greek. Koine Greek is a dialect preserved and known through thousands of papyrus writings reflecting all aspects of daily life. The Koine dialect added many vernacular expressions to classical Greek, thus making it more cosmopolitan. Simplifying the grammar also better adapted it to a worldwide culture. The new language, reflecting simple, popular speech, became the common language of commerce and diplomacy. The Greek language lost much of its elegance and finely shaded nuances as a result of its evolution from classic to Koine. Nevertheless, it retained its distinguishing characteristics of strength, beauty, clarity, and logical rhetorical power.

As has already been mentioned, during the centuries immediately before Christ, the Hebrew Scriptures were translated into Greek. This Greek translation, known as the Septuagint, helped introduce Greek forms of thought into Judaism and later into Christianity. Greek expressions acquired new and extended meanings in the Septuagint. Thus, the Greek Old Testament was very significant in the development of Christian thought. Often the usage of a Greek word in the Septuagint provides a key to its meaning in the New Testament.

Although most New Testament authors were Jewish, they wrote in Greek, the universal language of their time. In addition, some of the New Testament writers appear to have been familiar with Greek thinking and philosophy. The apostle John reflects this in the opening chapter to his Gospel. The apostle Paul also was acquainted with Greek authors (see Acts 17:28; 1 Corinthians 15:32; Titus 1:12). Thus Greek orators and philosophers influenced the New Testament writers, as did Hebrew prophets and scholars. At the same time, certain Greek words took on richer, more spiritual meanings in the context of the New Testament.

This unique assortment of elements from Koine Greek, Greek philosophy, the Septuagint, Jewish/Semitic thought, and Christianity combined to form a fairly unique New Testament language (once believed by medieval scholars to be a special "Holy Ghost" language). Tens of thousands of papyri unearthed in Egypt in the early twentieth century furnish lexical and grammatical parallels to biblical language, revealing that it was part of the linguistic fabric of that era.

THE NEW TESTAMENT TEXT AND MANUSCRIPTS

Christians began to make copies of the New Testament writings before the end of the first century. The early Christians were among the first to use the form of a book called a *codex,* instead of a scroll. A codex was constructed much like our modern books, by folding sheets of papyrus or vellum (treated animal hide) in the middle and then sewing them together at the spine. This kind of book was advantageous because (1) it enabled the scribe to write on both sides; (2) it facilitated easier access to particular passages (as opposed to a scroll, which had to be unrolled); (3) it enabled Christians to bind together all four Gospels or all of Paul's epistles or any other such combination; and (4) it made it easier for any individual or local church to make its own volume or portion of the New Testament.

Because none of the original documents (autographs) of the New Testament books still exist, we depend on copies for the text. Since copies had to be made by hand until the fifteenth century, occasionally errors or changes were introduced into the text by those who were copying them. The changes were then passed on to other copies that were made from those copies. At the same time, the earlier copies were lost or destroyed, so there was no way to know for certain what the original text was. The text that had been handed down to us was all we had—until the nineteenth century.

During the nineteenth and twentieth centuries (although one ancient codex had been brought to England in 1630), many ancient copies of various New Testament books have been found, and these have helped scholars reconstruct what is most likely the original text of these books. These discoveries are significant not only because their texts differ somewhat from our existing text but also because they were copied extremely early. This means that there was less time for errors to accumulate in the texts of these manuscripts, so theoretically, they should be closer to the original text.

One of these discoveries was a fragment called P52, which, according to most scholars, is the closest copy to an autograph that we have. It is dated around A.D. 110–125 and contains John 18:31-34, 37-38. This fragment, only twenty to thirty years removed from the autograph, was part of one of the earliest copies of John's Gospel. Another manuscript, known as the Chester Beatty Papyrus II, contains all of Paul's epistles except the Pastoral Epistles. This manuscript, designated P46, has been dated in the late first century. If this dating is accurate, then we have an entire collection of Paul's epistles that must have been made only twenty to thirty years after Paul wrote most of the Epistles. We possess many other early copies of various parts of the New Testament. Several of the papyrus manuscripts are dated from the late second century to the early fourth century. Some of the most important New Testament manuscripts are as follows:

The Oxyrhynchus Papyri
Beginning in 1898 Grenfell and Hunt discovered thousands of papyrus fragments in the ancient rubbish heaps of Oxyrhynchus, Egypt. This site yielded volumes of papyrus fragments containing all sorts of written material (literature, business and legal contracts, letters, etc.) as well as over sixty manuscripts containing portions of the New Testament. Some of the more noteworthy Oxyrhynchus papyrus manuscripts are P1 (Matthew 1), P5 (John 1, 16), P13 (Hebrews 2–5; 10–12), P22 (John 15–16), P39 (John 8), P77 (Matthew 23), P90 (John 18–19), P104 (Matthew 21), and P115 (Revelation 2–13).

The Chester Beatty Papyri (named after the owner, Chester Beatty)
These manuscripts were purchased from a dealer in Egypt during the 1930s by Chester Beatty and by the University of Michigan. The three manuscripts in this collection are very early and contain a large portion of the New Testament text. P45 (third century) contains portions of all four Gospels and Acts; P46 (second century) has almost all of Paul's epistles and Hebrews; and P47 (third century) contains Revelation 9–17.

The Bodmer Papyri (named after the owner, M. Martin Bodmer)

These manuscripts were purchased from a dealer in Egypt during the 1950s and 1960s. The three important papyri in this collection are P66 (about 175, containing almost all of John), P72 (third century, having all of 1 and 2 Peter and Jude), and P75 (about 200, containing large parts of Luke 3—John 15). P75 is thought to be one of the most accurate copies of Scripture.

Codex Sinaiticus

Constantin von Tischendorf discovered this manuscript in Saint Catherine's Monastery, which is situated at the foot of Mount Sinai, in the middle of the nineteenth century. The manuscript dates around A.D. 350, contains the entire New Testament, and provides an early and fairly reliable witness to the New Testament text.

Codex Vaticanus

This manuscript had been in the Vatican's library since at least 1481, but it was not made available to scholars, like Tischendorf and Tregelles, until the middle of the nineteenth century. This codex, dated slightly earlier than Sinaiticus, has both the Old Testament and New Testament in Greek, excluding the last part of the New Testament (from Hebrews 9:15 to the end of Revelation) and the Pastoral Epistles. For the most part, scholars have commended Codex Vaticanus for being one of the most trustworthy witnesses to the New Testament text.

Codex Alexandrinus

This is a fifth-century manuscript, displaying nearly all of the New Testament. It is known to be a very reliable witness to the General Epistles and Revelation.

Codex Ephraemi Rescriptus

This is a fifth-century document containing a large portion of the New Testament. It was partially erased and written upon with the sermons of St. Ephraem and then later deciphered by the painstaking efforts of Tischendorf.

Codex Bezae

This is a fifth-century manuscript named after Theodore Beza, its discoverer. It contains the Gospels and Acts and displays a text quite different from the manuscripts mentioned above.

Codex Washingtonianus (or, The Freer Gospels—named after its owner, Charles Freer)

This is a fifth-century manuscript containing all four Gospels. It is housed in the Smithsonian Institution in Washington, D.C.

By looking at the manuscripts, scholars have been able to reconstruct a general history of New Testament textual transmission (that is, the copying of the New Testament text).

It appears that in the early period of the church the New Testament text was copied with wild enthusiasm by novice and scholar alike. Novice copyists were prone to make errors. We have examples of many such copies, which could be labeled as "popular" texts. However, certain scribes in Alexandria and/or scribes familiar with Alexandrian scriptoral practices were responsible for maintaining a relatively pure text throughout the second, third, and fourth centuries.

The "early Alexandrian" text is reflected in many second- and third-century manuscripts. On the top of the list is P75 (about 175), the work of a competent and careful scribe. Not far behind in quality is P4 + P64 + P67 (about 150), the work of an excellent copyist. Other extremely good copies are P1 (middle third),

P20 (early third century), P23 (about 200), P27 (third century), P28 (third century), P32 (about 150–175), P39 (third century), P46 (about 125–150), P49 + P65 (third century), P66 (in its corrected form—P66^c; about 150), P70 (third century), P77 (about 150), P87 (about 125), P90 (about 175), and P91 (about 200). The "later Alexandrian" text, which displays editorial polishing, is exhibited in a few manuscripts, such as Codex Sinaiticus (fourth century), Codex Borgianus (fifth century), Codex Regius (eighth century), 33 (ninth century), 1739 (a tenth-century manuscript copied from a fourth-century Alexandrian manuscript much like P46), and manuscript 579 (thirteenth century).

At the end of the third century, another kind of Greek text came into being and then grew in popularity until it became the dominant text-type throughout Christendom. This is the text-type first produced by Lucian of Antioch, according to Jerome (in Jerome's introduction to his Latin translation of the Gospels). Lucian's text was a definite recension (i.e., a purposely created edition), as opposed to the Alexandrian text-type, which was produced by scribes who used and compared many manuscripts to preserve the best text. Of course, the Alexandrians did do some copyediting and grammatical polishing. By contrast, however, Lucian's text is the culmination of the popular text. That is, he removed awkward grammatical constructions and harmonized passages that differed in various manuscripts. Lucian (and/or his associates) must have used many different kinds of manuscripts of varying qualities to produce a harmonized, substantively edited New Testament text.

Lucian's text was produced prior to the persecution that came under the emperor Diocletian (about 303), during which time many copies of the New Testament were confiscated and destroyed. Not long after this period of devastation, Constantine came to power and then recognized Christianity as the state religion. There was, of course, a great need for copies of the New

Testament to be made and distributed to churches throughout
the Mediterranean world. It was at this time that Lucian's text
began to be propogated by bishops going out from the Antiochan
school to churches throughout the East, taking the text with
them. Lucian's text soon became the standard text of the Eastern
church and formed the basis for what is now called the
Byzantine text.

As the years went by, there were less and less Alexandrian
manuscripts produced, and more and more Byzantine manuscripts manufactured. Very few Egyptians continued to read
Greek (with the exception of those in Saint Catherine's Monastery, the site of the discovery of Codex Sinaiticus), and the rest
of the Mediterannean world turned to Latin. It was only those in
the Greek-speaking churches in Greece and Byzantium (modern
day Istanbul) that continued to make copies of the Greek text.
For century after century—from the sixth to the fourteenth—the
great majority of New Testament manuscripts were produced in
Byzantium, all bearing the same kind of text.

At present, we have more than six thousand manuscript copies
of the Greek New Testament or portions thereof. No other work
of Greek literature can boast of such numbers. Homer's *Iliad,* the
most copied of all Greek classical works, is extant in about 650
manuscripts. Euripides' tragedies exist in about 330 manuscripts.
The numbers on all the other works of Greek literature are far
less. Furthermore, it must be said that the amount of time
between the original composition and the next surviving manuscript is far less for the New Testament than for any other work
in Greek literature. The lapse for most classical Greek works is
about eight hundred to a thousand years, whereas the lapse for
many books in the New Testament is around one hundred years.
Because of the abundant wealth of manuscripts and because
several of the manuscripts are dated in the early centuries of the
church, New Testament textual scholars have a great advantage

over classical textual scholars. The New Testament scholars have the resources to reconstruct the original text of the New Testament with great accuracy, and they have produced some excellent editions of the Greek New Testament.

Finally, it must be said that although there are certainly differences in many of the New Testament manuscripts, not one fundamental doctrine of the Christian faith rests on a disputed reading. Frederic Kenyon, a renowned paleographer and textual critic, affirmed this when he said, "The Christian can take the whole Bible in his hand and say without fear or hesitation that he holds in it the true Word of God, handed down without essential loss from generation to generation throughout the centuries" (*Our Bible and the Ancient Manuscripts* [New York: Harper and Row, 1958], 55).

MODERN EDITIONS OF THE GREEK NEW TESTAMENT

The first printed edition of the Greek New Testament was the Complutensian Polyglot, published in Spain in 1514. In the same year, the renowned scholar Desiderius Erasmus was approached by a well-known publisher, Johann Froben, during the years 1514–1515 to produce a manuscript of the Greek New Testament for printing. When Erasmus compiled this text (published about 1525), he used five or six very late Byzantine manuscripts dating from the tenth to the thirteenth century. These manuscripts were far inferior to earlier manuscripts.

Erasmus's edition, with various alterations, became published again and again by different printers. The printer Robert Estienne eventually printed one such edition, which became known as the Textus Receptus ("the text received by all"—as it says in the preface). This edition became the standard Greek New Testament for several centuries until it was superseded by superior editions of the Greek New Testament, compiled from superior manuscript evidence.

As was already mentioned, beginning in the seventeenth century, earlier manuscripts were discovered—manuscripts with a text that differed from that found in the Textus Receptus. Around 1630, Codex Alexandrinus was brought to England. Two hundred years later, a German scholar named Constantin von Tischendorf discovered Codex Sinaiticus in Saint Catherine's Monastery (located near Mount Sinai). The earliest vellum manuscript, Codex Vaticanus, was made available to scholars in the middle of the nineteenth century. Other early and important manuscripts were discovered in the nineteenth century. Through the tireless labors of people like Constantin von Tischendorf, Samuel Tregelles, and F. H. A. Scrivener, manuscripts such as Codex Ephraemi Rescriptus, Codex Zacynthius, and Codex Augiensis were deciphered, collated, and published.

As the various manuscripts were discovered and made public, certain scholars labored to compile a Greek text that would more closely represent the original text than did the Textus Receptus. Around 1700, John Mill produced an improved Textus Receptus, and in the 1730s, Johannes Albert Bengel (known as the father of modern textual and philological studies in the New Testament) published a text that deviated from the Textus Receptus according to the evidence of earlier manuscripts.

In the 1800s, certain scholars began to abandon the Textus Receptus. Karl Lachman, a classical philologist, produced a fresh text (in 1831) that represented the fourth-century manuscripts. Samuel Tregelles (self-taught in Latin, Hebrew, and Greek), devoted his entire life's work to publishing one Greek text (which came out in six parts, from 1857 to 1872). As is stated in the introduction to this work, Tregelles' goal was "to exhibit the text of the New Testament in the very words in which it has been transmitted on the evidence of ancient authority." During this same era, Tischendorf was devoting a lifetime of labor to discovering manuscripts and producing accurate editions of the Greek New Testament. In a letter to his fiancée, he wrote, "I am confronted with a sacred task, the struggle to regain the original form of the New Testament." In fulfillment of his desire, he discovered Codex Sinaiticus, deciphered the palimpsest (meaning the text was erased and written over) Codex Ephraemi Rescriptus, collated countless manuscripts, and produced several editions of the Greek New Testament (the eighth edition is the best).

Aided by the work of the previous scholars, two British scholars, Brooke Westcott and Fenton Hort, worked together for twenty-eight years to produce a volume entitled *The New Testament in the Original Greek* (1881). Along with this publication, they made known their theory (which was chiefly Hort's) that Codex Vaticanus and Codex Sinaiticus (along with a few other early manuscripts) represented a text that most closely replicated the original writing.

The nineteenth century was a fruitful era for the recovery of the Greek New Testament; the twentieth century, no less so. Those living in the twentieth century have witnessed the publication of the Oxyrhynchus Papyri, the Chester Beatty Papyri, and the Bodmer Papyri. To date, there are 115 papyri containing portions of the New Testament—several of which date from the late first century to the early fourth century. These significant discoveries, providing scholars with many ancient manuscripts, have greatly enhanced the effort to recover the original wording of the New Testament.

At the beginning of the twentieth century, Eberhard Nestle used the best editions of the Greek New Testament produced in the nineteenth century to compile a text that represented the majority consensus. The work of making new editions was carried on by his son for several years and then came under the care of Kurt Aland. The latest edition (the twenty-seventh) of Nestle-Aland's *Novum Testamentum Graece* appeared in 1993. The same Greek text appears in another popular volume published by the United Bible Societies, called the *Greek New Testament* (fourth edition). Aland has argued that the Nestle-Aland text, twenty-seventh edition (NA^{27}), comes closer to the original text of the New Testament than did Tischendorf or Westcott and Hort. Though some scholars disagree with Aland, most consider the twenty-seventh edition of the Nestle-Aland text to represent the latest and best in textual scholarship.

Ancient Versions
of the Bible

TRANSLATIONS OF THE HEBREW BIBLE
. . . .

The process of Bible translation began before the birth of Christ, with translations of the Old Testament being made into Greek and Aramaic. Many of the dispersed Jews who lived prior to the coming of Christ did not know Hebrew and therefore needed a translation in Greek or Aramaic.

The Septuagint

As was mentioned earlier, the first known translation of the Hebrew Old Testament into Greek was the Septuagint. It was the Bible of Jesus' apostles, the version from which most Old Testament quotations in the New Testament come, and the Bible of the early church as far as the Old Testament was concerned.

According to tradition, the Septuagint Pentateuch was translated by a team of seventy scholars in Alexandria, Egypt. (Hence its common designation LXX, the Roman numeral for seventy.) The Jewish community in Egypt spoke Greek, not Hebrew, so a Greek translation of the Old Testament was needed by that community of Jews. The exact date of translation is not known, but evidence indicates that the Septuagint Pentateuch was completed in the third century B.C. The rest of the Old Testament was probably translated over a long period of time, as it clearly represents the work of many different scholars. Thus, the Septuagint is not a single version but a collection of versions made by various translators, who differed greatly in their methods and their knowledge of Hebrew. The translations of the individual books are in no way uniform. Many books are translated very literally, while others, like Job and Daniel, are quite free, or dynamic.

Other Greek Versions

Because of the broad acceptance and use of the Septuagint among Christians, the Jews renounced it in favor of a number of other Greek versions. Aquila, a proselyte and disciple of a prominent rabbi named Akiba ben Joseph, produced a new translation around A.D. 130. In the spirit of his teacher, Aquila produced an extremely literal translation, often to the point of communicating poorly in Greek. This literal approach, however, gained the version wide acceptance among Jews. Only fragments of this version have survived, but its literal nature reveals much about its Hebrew textual base.

A man named Symmachus produced a new version around A.D. 170, designed not only for accuracy but also to communicate well in the Greek language. His version has survived only in a few fragments of the *Hexapla* (see below).

Another Greek version came from Theodotian, a Jewish proselyte from the end of the second century A.D. His version was apparently a revision of an earlier Greek version, possibly the Septuagint. This version has only survived in a few early Christian quotations, though it was once widely used.

Origen's *Hexapla*

The Christian theologian Origen (about A.D. 185–255) arranged the Old Testament with six parallel translations for comparison in his *Hexapla*. In his effort to find the best text of the Septua-

gint, Origen wrote out six parallel columns containing first the
Hebrew, second the Hebrew transliterated into Greek characters,
third the text of Aquila, fourth the text of Symmachus, fifth his
own corrected Septuagint text, and sixth the text of Theodotian.
Jerome used this great Bible at Caesarea in his work on the
Vulgate (after A.D. 382—see below). Almost four centuries after
Origen's death, a Mesopotamian bishop, Paul of Tella, also used
the *Hexapla* in the library at Caesarea (A.D. 616–617) to make a
translation into Syriac of Origen's fifth column, the corrected
Septuagint. Then in A.D. 638 the Islamic hordes swept through
Caesarea, and the *Hexapla* disappeared. Other than a few frag-
ments, only Bishop Paul's Syriac translation of Origen's fifth
column remains.

Early Christian Versions
As the gospel spread and churches multiplied in the early centuries of the Christian era, Christians in various countries wanted
to read the Bible in their own languages. As a result, as early as
the second century, many translations were made in several different languages. For example, there were translations done in
Coptic for the Egyptians, in Syriac for those whose language
was Aramaic, in Armenian for the Armenians, in Gothic for the
Germanic people called the Goths, and in Latin for the Romans
and Carthagenians.

Latin translations, however, were far more predominant than
all other translations, as most of the world became dominated by
the Roman Catholic church. The most famous Latin translation
was done by Jerome around A.D. 400. This translation, known
as the Latin Vulgate (*vulgate* meaning "common"—hence, the
Latin text for the common person), was used extensively in the
Roman Catholic church for many centuries. As far as we know,
the first English versions were based on the Latin Vulgate.

Latin Versions

As we have mentioned, in the early days of the Roman Empire and the church, Greek was the language of Christians. Even the first leaders of the church in Rome wrote and preached in Greek. But as the Roman Empire and the church aged, Latin began to win out, especially in the West. So it was only natural that Christians began translating the Greek New Testament and Septuagint into Latin. One of the earliest Latin versions was called the Old Latin Bible. No complete manuscript of it survives. Much of the Old Testament and most of the New, however, can be reconstructed from quotations by the early church fathers. Around A.D. 160, Tertullian apparently used a Latin version of the Scriptures. Not long after this, the Old Latin text seems to have been in circulation, evidenced by Cyprian's use of it before his death in A.D. 258. Consequently, scholars think an Old Latin Bible was in circulation in Carthage in North Africa as early as A.D. 250. From the surviving fragments and quotations, there seem to have been two types of Old Latin texts, the African and the European.

Around the third century A.D., Latin began to replace Greek as the language of learning in the larger Roman world. A uniform, reliable Bible text was needed for theological and liturgical uses. To fill this need, Pope Damasus I (A.D. 336–384) commissioned Jerome, an eminent scholar in Latin, Greek, and Hebrew, to create such a translation.

Jerome completed the Gospels in A.D. 383; Acts and the rest of the New Testament eventually followed. The Gospels were a thorough and painstaking retranslation based on the European Old Latin and an Alexandrian Greek text. The rest of the New Testament, however, was a much more limited effort, with the Old Latin remaining dominant unless the Greek text demanded change. No one is sure if the rest of the New Testament was the work of Jerome himself.

Soon after Jerome completed Psalms, Pope Damasus died, and

Jerome's efforts were no longer undergirded by the hierarchy of the church. So Jerome eventually made his way to a monastery in Bethlehem, where he continued his translation work—often against strong opposition. Using the *Hexapla* of Origen, Jerome had access to the Septuagint. From that he translated into Latin the books of Job, 1 and 2 Chronicles, Proverbs, Ecclesiastes, and Song of Songs. He also translated Psalms again. This version of Psalms came to be known as the *Gallican Psalter,* an important part of Roman Catholic liturgy and breviary. Later, Jerome quit using the Greek Old Testament and began translating from the original Hebrew texts around A.D. 389; he completed his Latin version of the Old Testament in A.D. 405.

Jerome did nearly all of his work by private initiative, so his translation was slow to be accepted by the church. The Old Latin version was extremely familiar and was not easily abandoned. In addition, the Greek church leaders held the Septuagint to be divinely inspired, so some leaders thought that the Vulgate would sever ties between the Latin and the Greek churches. Jerome was stubborn, however, and held out against all his critics. In time the Vulgate was accepted, and by the middle of the sixth century a complete Bible within a single cover was in use. This contained Jerome's Old Testament, his *Gallican Psalter,* his translations of Tobit and Judith (both books of the Apocrypha), and his revision of the Gospels. Older Latin versions completed his New Testament. These may also have been revised by Jerome.

Only very gradually did the Vulgate replace the Old Latin Bible. It took a thousand years before the Vulgate was made the official Roman Catholic Bible (by the Council of Trent in 1546). That council also authorized an official, corrected edition, which was first issued by Pope Sixtus V (1585–1590) in 1590 in three volumes. It proved unpopular, however, and Pope Clement VIII (1592–1605) recalled it and issued a new official Vulgate in 1592, which has been the standard edition to recent times.

Coptic

Coptic, an Egyptian language, was the language of the native
populations who lived along the length of the Nile River. It was
never overtaken by the Greek of Alexander and his generals or
even threatened by the Latin of the Caesars. Its script is composed of twenty-five Greek capital letters and seven cursive
letters taken over from Egyptian writing to express sounds not
in the Greek.

Through the centuries it developed at least five main dialects:
Achmimic, sub-Achmimic, Sahidic, Fayumic, and Bohairic.
Fragments of biblical material have been found in all five dialects. They gradually faded out of use until—by the eleventh
century—only Bohairic, the language of the Delta, and Sahidic,
the language of Upper (Southern) Egypt, remained. They too,
however, had become strictly religious languages used only in
Coptic churches by the seventeenth century because of the long
dominance of Arabic that began with the Islamic conquest of
Egypt in A.D. 641.

The earliest translation was in Sahidic in Upper Egypt, where
Greek was less universally understood. The Sahidic Old and
New Testaments were probably completed by around A.D. 200.
Greek was so much more dominant in the Delta that the transla-
tion of the Scriptures into Bohairic probably was not completed
until somewhat later. Since Bohairic was the language of the
Delta, however, it was also the language of the Coptic Patriarch
in Alexandria. When the Patriarchate moved from Alexandria
to Cairo in the eleventh century, the Bohairic texts went along.
Bohairic gradually became the major religious language of the
Coptic church. The Copts had separated from the Roman Catholic church over doctrinal issues after the Council of Chalcedon in
A.D. 451 and had then been isolated from Western Christendom
by centuries of Islamic rule.

Syriac

One of the family of Semitic languages, Syriac was the predominant tongue of the region of Edessa and western Mesopotamia. The version known today as the Peshitta Bible (still the official Bible of Christians of the old Assyrian area churches) developed through several stages. One of the most famous and widely used translations in the early church was the Syriac Diatessaron, done by Tatian, a man who had been a disciple of Justin Martyr at Rome. The Diatessaron, Tatian's harmony of the Gospels translated from the Greek about A.D. 170, was very popular among Syriac-speaking Christians. Syrian bishops had an uphill battle getting Christians to use *The Gospel of the Separated Ones* (meaning the text in which the four Gospels were separated from one another rather than blended) in their churches.

Other portions of the Bible were also put into Old Syriac. Quotations from the church fathers indicate that some type of second-century Old Syriac text existed along with the Diatessaron. In fact, the Old Testament may have been a Jewish translation into Syriac, which Syrian Christians made their own, just as Greek Christians had done with the Septuagint. It then underwent a more or less official revision around the end of the fourth century, emerging as the Peshitta (meaning "basic" or "simple") text.

Armenian

Christians from Syria carried their faith to their Armenian neighbors in eastern Asia Minor. As early as the third century, with the conversion of Tiridates III (who reigned from 259 to 314), Armenia became a Christian kingdom—the first in history. Sometime during the fifth century, an Armenian alphabet was created so that the Bible could be translated into the language of these new believers. The Armenian translation is considered one of the most beautiful and accurate ancient versions

59

of the Greek. An old tradition says that the New Testament was the work of Mesrop (a bishop in Armenia, 390–439), who is credited with inventing both the Armenian and Georgian alphabets.

Gothic Translation of Ulfilas

Ulfilas grew up in Constantinople, the Roman Empire's eastern capital. Here he received his education and began his life of service to the church. In 341 Eusebius of Nicomedia, bishop of Constantinople, consecrated Ulfilas as bishop. Soon afterward the young bishop proceeded to Dacia (north of the Danube River), and for his remaining years he served as the church's principal missionary to the western Goths in this region. The many converts indicate that Ulfilas's efforts to spread the gospel had extensive results. After several years, persecution forced Ulfilas out of Dacia, and his work thereafter originated from a residence in Moesia (south of the Danube River), an area within the Empire's borders.

Ulfilas's move to Moesia prompted the beginnings of the project for which he is best remembered. This was his translation of the Old and New Testaments into the Goths' vernacular language. Toward this end Ulfilas first had to reduce Gothic speech to writing, a task involving the invention of an alphabet based on Greek. Ulfilas appears to have translated the whole New Testament. This translation, as reflected in later editions, was apparently quite literal and dependant on the early Byzantine text. He also translated most of the Old Testament.

English Versions
of the Bible

Before we discuss the various English versions of the Bible that have been created, we should first examine a few issues related to translation.

Since few people today are able to understand Hebrew, Aramaic, and Greek (the languages in which the Bible was originally written), it has been necessary to translate the Scriptures into the language of the people. In other words, the message of the original languages has been rendered in an understandable way in another language. English, of course, is one of the languages into which the Scriptures were translated.

As anyone who has learned to speak two different languages has discovered, however, there is no single way to translate something from one language into another. There are many different shades of meaning that can be communicated in all sorts of ways. Some shades of meaning can be lost or obscured by certain translation methods, while other methods make them more clear. Many considerations and decisions must be made when making a translation; inevitably some things will be lost in the process and others gained.

If we look at Bible translation in the simplest of terms, there are two basic methods. The first is called "formal equivalence" (meaning word-for-word); the second is called "functional equivalence" or "dynamic equivalence" (meaning thought-for-thought). In doing a formal-equivalence translation, the translator attempts to retain as much of the specific wording of the original languages (Hebrew or Greek) as possible when rendering a sentence into the language he or she is working with (in this case, English). In doing a functional-equivalence translation, the translator tries to convey the *thoughts* of the original languages into the closest natural equivalent in English. This approach places a greater emphasis upon meaning and style than a word-for-word approach does when rendering a sentence in English. The goal of this kind of translation is for a passage to have the same impact upon today's English readers that the original had upon its audience.

The truth of the matter is that not one English translation is either completely word-for-word or completely thought-for-thought. Translations are usually a mixture, with tendencies toward one method or the other.

Most of the older English translations tended to be literal (word-for-word) translations of the original languages. Some modern translations have continued this trend toward literalness. Some of these translators have preferred the literal approach to guard against misrepresenting the text in an attempt to make it more clear. This is a constant danger with thought-for-thought translations, because the more freedom a translator is given in rendering a phrase, the more subjective the process becomes. The thought-for-thought translator must try, in a sense, to enter into the mind of the author. And who can always know with certainty what the author's original intended meaning was? For this reason, a thought-for-thought translation is usually done with the cooperation of a large group of Bible scholars.

It should be said that the fact that a word-for-word rendering can be executed more consistently than a thought-for-thought one can does not make it inherently better. There are also disadvantages to literal translations, especially with respect to readability. Often sentences are rendered in a way that is simply not natural for an English reader, because the translator is reflecting Hebrew or Greek word order and not English. Another casualty from this method is that much of the emotive quality of the original text is lost in translation. In short, literal translations make great study Bibles (because of their consistency of wording) but poor reading Bibles (because of their lack of readability and emotive quality). Because of this, an increasing number of translators in this century have turned to the thought-for-thought approach in an attempt to produce translations that are both reliable and readable—that is, they reliably convey the meaning of the text without sacrificing its readability.

THE FIRST TRANSLATIONS INTO ENGLISH

The long and fascinating history of the English Bible begins as early as the seventh century. Christianity had spread to London, England, by the third century, and it is possible that the Bible was translated into the native language of the people there, but we have no record of this. We do know that missionaries from Rome brought the Latin Vulgate (the official translation of the Roman church) to England as early as the fifth century. Christians living in England at that time depended on monks for any kind of instruction from the Bible, and these monks read and taught the Latin Vulgate. After a few centuries, more monasteries were founded, and the need arose for translations of the Bible in English. The earliest English translation, as far as we know, was one done by a seventh-century monk named Caedmon, who made a metrical, or poetic, version of parts of the Old and New Testaments. Another English churchman named Bede is said to have translated the Gospels into English. Tradition has it that he was translating the Gospel of John on his deathbed in 735. King Alfred the Great, a very literate king who reigned from 871–899, included in his laws parts of the Ten Commandments translated into English, and he also translated the Psalms.

The most famous Bible from this period is the Lindisfarne Gospels (950). This work contains alternating lines of Latin text and Anglo-Saxon translation.

In the late tenth century, Aelfric (about 955–1020), abbot of Eynsham, made idiomatic translations of various parts of the Bible. Two of these translations still exist. Later, in the 1300s, William of Shoreham translated Psalms into English, as did Richard Rolle, whose editions included verse-by-verse commentary. Both of these translations were metrical and were therefore called Psalters. These translations were popular when John Wycliffe was a young man.

John Wycliffe (about 1329–1384), the most eminent Oxford theologian of his day, and his associates were the first to translate the entire Bible from Latin into English. Wycliffe's motivation to translate the Bible stemmed partly from his theological battles with the pope. Wycliffe believed that the pope's decrees had to be grounded in Scripture, otherwise they held no authority. This emphasis on the importance of comparing church teaching against the Scriptures led to the need for an understandable translation of the Bible. Wycliffe and his associates completed the New Testament around 1380 and the Old Testament in 1382.

THE REFORMATION

William Tyndale can be considered the father of most modern English translations, because (1) he was the first to translate the Bible from the original languages (a practice that has now become standard policy), (2) many standard versions find their roots in his work, and (3) almost all other English translations have at least been influenced by Tyndale's work and by the myriad of translations that he spawned.

Translations of the Bible prior to the work of William Tyndale were done from the Latin text, which was itself a translation of the original Greek and Hebrew texts of the Bible. With the dawn of the Renaissance, however, renewed interest in the classics made the Greek and Hebrew texts available once again. By translating from the original languages, Tyndale helped to improve the accuracy of English Bibles and set a new standard for Bible translation.

The influence of Tyndale's work was also greatly increased by the invention of the printing press a few decades earlier. The printing press enabled Tyndale's work to be *owned* by the layperson as well as understood by him or her.

Tyndale himself was only able to complete the New Testament, although he translated several Old Testament books as well. While Tyndale was in prison on charges of heresy (he was eventually strangled and burned at the stake), an associate of his named Miles Coverdale (1488–1569) brought to completion an entire Bible in English—based largely on Tyndale's translation of the New Testament and other Old Testament books.

Tyndale's work (completed by Coverdale) was the opening of the dike. Since then, there has been a virtual flood of English Bible versions. Among the most noteworthy of the Reformation period are Thomas Matthew's Version: the Great Bible (1538), the Geneva Bible (1550), the Bishops' Bible (1568), and the Douai-Reims Bible (1582, 1609–1610). These works prepared the way for the Authorized King James Version (KJV or AV) of 1611—a translation that has captured the attention of the English-speaking world even to this day.

The King James Version was the product of a group of scholars commissioned by King James. They were instructed to follow the text of the Bishops' Bible while consulting other translations (Tyndale's, the Geneva Bible, etc.) to obtain the most accurate reading. Once it was completed, the Authorized King James Version became the standard version of England and the English-speaking world for many centuries, and its resulting influence upon the English language and culture is incalculable.

THE EIGHTEENTH AND NINETEENTH CENTURIES

The King James Bible continued to reign as the standard English Bible throughout the eighteenth century, but by the nineteenth century, the King James Version's deficiencies were becoming increasingly apparent to scholars.

First, knowledge of Hebrew and Greek was very limited in the early seventeenth century. By the nineteenth century, many advances in linguistic studies had enriched and sharpened the scholars' understanding of Hebrew and Greek grammar and vocabulary.

Second, as was discussed in chapter three, manuscript discoveries in the eighteenth and nineteenth centuries spawned new editions of the Greek New Testament. The Greek text underlying the New Testament of the King James Version was the Textus Receptus (see chapter 3, "How We Got the New Testament"), a text that is probably less accurate to the original than those that had since become available.

The King James translators had done well with the resources that were available to them, but by the nineteenth century, the limitations of those resources were becoming very apparent to many scholars.

By the latter part of the nineteenth century, the Christian community had been given three very good Greek New Testament texts: Tregelles', Tischendorf's, and Westcott and Hort's. And as was mentioned earlier, the scholarly community had accumulated more knowledge about the meaning of various Hebrew words and Greek words. Therefore, there was a great need for a new English translation based upon a better text—and with more accurate renderings of the original languages.

A few individuals attempted to meet this need. In 1871, John Nelson Darby, leader of the Plymouth Brethren movement, produced a translation called the *New Translation,* which was largely based on Codex Vaticanus and Codex Sinaiticus. In 1872, J. B. Rotherham published a translation of Tregelles' text, in which he attempted to reflect the emphasis inherent in the Greek text. This translation is still being published under the title *The Emphasized Bible.* And in 1875, Samuel Davidson produced a New Testament translation of Tischendorf's text.

The first major corporate effort was initiated in 1870 by the Convocation of Canterbury, which decided to sponsor a major revision of the King James Version. Sixty-five British scholars, working in various committees, made significant changes to the King James Version. The Old Testament scholars corrected mistranslations of Hebrew words and reformatted poetic passages into poetic form. The New Testament scholars made thousands of changes based upon better textual evidence. Their goal was to make the New Testament revision reflect not the Textus Receptus but the texts of Tregelles, Tischendorf, and Westcott and Hort. When the complete Revised Version appeared in 1885, it was received with great enthusiasm. Over 3 million copies sold in the first year of its publication. Its popularity was not long lasting, however, as most people continued to prefer the King James Version over all other translations.

Several American scholars had been invited to join the revision work, with the understanding that any of their suggestions not accepted by the British scholars would appear in an appendix. Furthermore, the American scholars had agreed not to publish their own American revision until fourteen years later. When the time

came (1901), the American Standard Version (ASV) was published
by several surviving members of the original American committee.
This translation, generally regarded as superior to the English
Revised Version, is an accurate, literal rendering of very trustworthy texts both in the Old Testament and the New Testaments.

MAJOR REVISIONS AND TRANSLATIONS
OF THE TWENTIETH CENTURY

The nineteenth century was a fruitful era for the Greek New Testament and subsequent English translations. It was also a century
in which Hebrew studies were greatly advanced. The twentieth
century has also been fruitful—especially for textual studies.
Those living in the twentieth century have witnessed the discovery of the Dead Sea Scrolls (see the discussion in chapter 2), the
Oxyrhynchus Papyri, the Chester Beatty Papyri, and the Bodmer
Papyri (see the discussion in chapter 3). These amazing discoveries, providing scholars with hundreds of ancient manuscripts,
have greatly enhanced the effort to recover the original wording
of the Old and New Testaments. At the same time, they have
prompted revisions to existing translations.

Revised Standard Version (RSV)
The organization that held the copyright to the American Standard Version, called the International Council of Religious Education, authorized a new revision in 1937. The New Testament
translators generally followed the seventeenth edition of the Nestle Text (1941), while the Old Testament translators followed the
Masoretic Text. Both groups, however, adopted readings from
other ancient sources when they were considered to be more
accurate. The New Testament was published in 1946, and the
entire Bible with the Old Testament in 1952.

The principles of the revision were specified in the preface
to the Revised Standard Version:

The Revised Standard Version is not a new translation in the language of today. It is not a paraphrase which aims at striking idioms. It is a revision which seeks to preserve all that is best in the English Bible as it has been known and used throughout the years.

This revision was well received by many Protestant churches and soon became their "standard" text. The Revised Standard Version was later published with the Apocrypha of the Old Testament (1957), in a Catholic Edition (1965), and in what is called the *Common Bible,* which includes the Old Testament, the New Testament, the Apocrypha, and the Deuterocanonical books, with international endorsements by Protestants, Greek Orthodox, and Roman Catholics.

Many evangelical Christians, however, did not receive the Revised Standard Version very well—primarily because of one verse, Isaiah 7:14, which reads, "Therefore the Lord himself will give you a sign. Behold, a young woman shall conceive and bear a son, and shall call his name Immanuel." Evangelicals contended that the text should read "virgin," not "young woman." As a result, the Revised Standard Version was panned, if not banned, by many Christians.

New American Standard Bible (NASB)

Dissatisfaction with the Revised Standard Version prompted evangelical scholars to produce their own revision of the American Standard Version. The Lockman Foundation, a nonprofit Christian corporation committed to evangelism, promoted this revision of the American Standard Version because "the producers of this translation were imbued with the conviction that interest in the American Standard Version 1901 should be renewed and increased" (from the introduction). Indeed, the American Standard Version was a monumental work of scholarship and a very accurate translation. However, its popularity was waning, and it was fast disappearing from the scene. Therefore, the Lockman Foundation organized a team of thirty-two scholars to prepare a new revision. These scholars, all committed to the inspiration of Scripture, strove to produce a literal translation of the Bible in the belief that such a translation brings the contemporary reader as close as possible to the actual wording and grammatical structure of the original writers.

The translators of the *New American Standard Bible* were instructed by the Lockman Foundation "to adhere to the original languages of the Holy Scriptures as closely as possible and at the same time to obtain a fluent and readable style according to current English usage." After the *New American Standard Bible* was published (1963 for the New Testament and 1971 for the entire Bible), it received a mixed response. Some critics applauded its literal accuracy, while others sharply criticized its language for hardly being contemporary or modern. On the whole, the *New American Standard Bible* became respected as a good study Bible that accurately reflects the wording of the original languages but that is lacking as a translation for Bible reading.

New Revised Standard Version (NRSV)
In due course, the time came for the Revised Standard Version to be further revised. This revision is called the New Revised Standard Version, published in 1990. Its history and heritage is stated explicitly in its introduction by Bruce Metzger, the chairperson of the revision committee:

> The New Revised Standard Version of the Bible is an authorized revision of the Revised Standard Version, published in 1952, which was a revision of the American Standard Version, published in 1901, which, in turn, embodied earlier revisions of the King James Version, published in 1611.

The need for issuing a revision of the Revised Standard Version of the Bible arises from three circumstances: (a) the acquisition of still older Biblical manuscripts, (b) further investigation of linguistic features of the text, and (c) changes in preferred English usage.

These three criteria specified by Metzger are essentially the same principles behind all revisions of Bible translations.

New International Version (NIV)

A century that has witnessed several revisions of the King James Version has also witnessed the first translation that outsold the King James Version since its inception. That translation is the New International Version, a completely new rendering of the original languages done by an international group of more than a hundred scholars. These scholars worked many years and in several committees to produce an excellent thought-for-thought translation in contemporary English for private and public use.

The translators of the New International Version sought to make a version that was midway between a literal rendering (as in the *New American Standard Bible*) and a free paraphrase (as in *The Living Bible* [TLB]). Their goal was to convey in English the thought of the original writers. This is succinctly explained in the original preface to the New Testament:

Certain convictions and aims guided the translators. They are all committed to the full authority and complete trustworthiness of the Scriptures. Therefore, their first concern was the accuracy of the translation and its fidelity to the thought of the New Testament writers. While they weighed the significance of the lexical and grammatical details of the Greek text, they have striven for more than a word-for-word translation. Because thought patterns and syntax differ from language to language, faithful communication of the meaning of the writers of the New Testament demanded frequent modifications in sentence structure and constant regard for the contextual meanings of words.

Concern for clarity of style—that it should be idiomatic without being idiosyncratic, contemporary without being dated—also motivated the translators and their consultants. They have consistently aimed at simplicity of expression, with sensitive attention to the connotation and sound of the chosen word. At the same time, they endeavored to avoid a sameness of style in order to reflect the varied styles and moods of the New Testament writers.

The New Testament of the New International Version was published in 1973, and the entire Bible in 1978. This version has been phenomenally successful. Millions upon millions of readers have adopted the New International Version as "their" Bible. Since 1987, it has outsold the King James Version, the best-seller for centuries—a remarkable indication of its popularity and acceptance in the Christian community. The New International Version, sponsored by the New York Bible Society and published by Zondervan Publishers, has become a standard version used for private reading and pulpit reading in many English-speaking countries.

Other Translations of the Twentieth Century

Because of the many textual and linguistic advances that continued to be made in the twentieth century, translation after translation continued to appear. New philosophies and theories of translation, such as the new emphasis upon "dynamic equivalence" (see the beginning of this chapter), also drove the production of these new translations.

Among the more noteworthy of the dynamic-equivalence translations to have been produced in the twentieth century are

The Twentieth Century New Testament, The New Testament in Modern Speech, The Complete Bible: An American Translation, Good News Bible: Today's English Version, The Living Bible, the Contemporary English Version (CEV), and the New Living Translation (NLT).

The Twentieth Century New Testament (1902) is a smooth-flowing, accurate, easy-to-read translation that captivates readers from start to finish. Born out of a desire to make the Bible readable and understandable, it is the product of the labors of a committee of twenty men and women who worked together over many years to construct a simple rendition of the Word of God.

The New Testament in Modern Speech (1903) was the work of Richard Weymouth. During his life, he spent time producing an edition of the Greek text (called *The Resultant Greek Testament,* published in 1862) that was more accurate than the Textus Receptus, and then he labored to produce an English translation of this Greek text in a modern-speech version. His translation was very well received; it has gone through several editions and many printings.

The Complete Bible: An American Translation is the earliest American modern-speech translation, produced by Edgar J. Goodspeed, professor of New Testament at the University of Chicago. When he made this translation (in 1923) he said that he wanted to give his version "something of the force and freshness that reside in the original Greek." He said, "I wanted my translation to make on the reader something of the impression the New Testament must have made on its earliest readers, and to invite the continuous reading of the whole book at a time."

The New Testament in Today's English Version, also known as *Good News for Modern Man,* was published by the American Bible Society in 1966. The translation was originally done by Robert Bratcher, a research associate of the Translations Department of the American Bible Society, and then further refined by the American

73

Bible Society. The translation, heavily promoted by several Bible societies and very affordable, sold more than 35 million copies within six years of the time of printing. Because of the success of the New Testament, the American Bible Society was asked by other Bible societies to make an Old Testament translation following the same principles used in the New Testament. The entire Bible was published in 1976, and is known as the *Good News Bible: Today's English Version.* A further development of this kind of translation done by the American Bible Society yielded the version known as the Contemporary English Version (1992).

In 1962, Kenneth Taylor published a paraphrase of the New Testament epistles in a volume called *Living Letters.* This new dynamic paraphrase, written in everyday English, became well received and widely acclaimed—especially for its ability to communicate the message of God's Word to the common person. The entire text of *The Living Bible* was published in 1971. *The Living Bible* was very popular among English readers worldwide. More than 40 million copies have been sold by the publishing house Taylor created specifically to publish *The Living Bible.* The company is called Tyndale House Publishers—named after William Tyndale, the father of modern English translations of the Bible.

With over 40 million copies in print, *The Living Bible* has been a very popular version of the Bible for more than thirty years. But various criticisms spurred Kenneth Taylor to produce a revision of his paraphrase. Under the sponsorship of Tyndale House Publishers, *The Living Bible* underwent a thorough revision. More than ninety evangelical scholars from various theological backgrounds and denominations worked for seven years to produce the New Living Translation. The scholars carefully revised the text of *The Living Bible* acccording to the most reliable editions of the Hebrew and Greek texts. The translation continues in Taylor's dynamic-equivalence tradition while improving many of *The Living Bible*'s deficiencies.

TIMELINE OF EVENTS

c. 2000 B.C.	The birth of Abraham
c. 1447 B.C.	The Exodus (early date)
c. 1400 B.C.	The Israelites enter the Promised Land (early date)
c. 1270 B.C.	The Exodus (late date)
c. 1230 B.C.	The Israelites enter the Promised Land (late date)
c. 1010 B.C.	David is crowned king of all the Israelite tribes
931 B.C.	The kingdom is divided into Israel and Judah
722 B.C.	Exile of the northern kingdom of Israel
597/586 B.C.	Exile of the southern kingdom of Judah
538 B.C.	Many Jews return from exile
516 B.C.	Completion of the Second Temple
457 B.C.	Ezra arrives in Jerusalem
444 B.C.	Nehemiah arrives in Jerusalem
c.160 B.C.	Judas Maccabeus dies
c. 6/5 B.C.	Jesus Christ is born
c. A.D. 30	Jesus' crucifixion and resurrection
c. A.D. 49	Council of Jerusalem
c. A.D. 60	Paul's imprisonment in Rome
A.D. 70	The destruction of the Temple in Jerusalem
c. A.D. 90	John the apostle is exiled to Patmos
A.D. 324	Constantine secures his rule over the Roman Empire
A.D. 395	The Roman Empire is divided into East and West
c. A.D. 400	Jerome completes the Latin Vulgate
A.D. 410	Barbarians attack Rome
A.D. 800	Charlemagne is crowned emperor of the Holy Roman Empire
c. A.D. 1008	Leningrad Codex is produced by the Masoretes
A.D. 1054	The church officially splits, separating Roman Catholicism from Eastern Orthodoxy
A.D. 1066	William of Normandy conquers England
c. A.D. 1450	Johannes Gutenberg invents his printing press

A.D. 1517	Martin Luther nails his Ninety-five Theses to the chapel door
A.D. 1534	Henry VIII establishes the Church of England
A.D. 1536	William Tyndale is strangled and burned at the stake
A.D. 1563	Council of Trent is adjourned
A.D. 1611	King James Version is completed
A.D. 1616	William Shakespeare dies
A.D. 1620	Pilgrims arrive in America
A.D. 1776	The American Revolution
A.D. 1881	Westcott and Hort publish their *Greek New Testament*
A.D. 1918	World War I ends
A.D. 1945	World War II ends
A.D. 1947	Discovery of the Dead Sea Scrolls

FOR FURTHER READING

Aland, Kurt, and Barbara Aland. *The Text of the New Testament.*
Grand Rapids: Eerdmans, 1988.

Bailey, Lloyd R. *The Word of God: A Guide to English Versions of
the Bible.* Louisville, Ky.: Westminster John Knox Press, 1982.

Bruce, F. F. *The Books and the Parchments.* Old Tappan, N.J.:
Fleming H. Revell Co., 1984.

Bruce, F. F. *The Canon of Scripture.* Grand Rapids: Eerdmans, 1988.

Bruce, F. F. *The History of the Bible in English: From the Earliest
Versions to Today.* New York: Oxford University Press, 1978.

The Cambridge History of the Bible. 3 vols. New York: Cambridge
University Press, 1975.

Comfort, Philip W. *The Origin of the Bible.* Wheaton, Ill.: Tyndale
House Publishers, 1992.

Comfort, Philip W., ed. *Early Manuscripts and Modern Translations
of the New Testament,* second edition. Grand Rapids: Baker Book
House, 1996.

Gamble, Harry Y. *Books and Readers in the Early Church.* New
Haven: Yale University Press, 1995.

Glassman, Eugene H. *The Translation Debate: What Makes a
Translation Good?* Downers Grove, Ill.: InterVarsity Press, 1981.

Hill, Andrew E., and John H. Walton. *A Survey of the Old Testament.*
Grand Rapids: Zondervan Publishing House, 1991.

Kubo, Sakae, and Walter Specht. *So Many Versions?* Revised and
enlarged ed. Grand Rapids: Zondervan Publishing House, 1983.

Lewis, Jack P. *The English Bible from KJV to NIV.* Grand Rapids:
Baker Book House, 1982.

Long, John D. *The Bible in English: John Wycliffe and William
Tyndale.* Lanham, Md.: University Press of America, 1998.

Metzger, Bruce M. *The New Testament: Its Background, Growth,
and Content.* Nashville: Abingdon Press, 1983.

Metzger, Bruce. *The Text of the New Testament,* second edition.
Oxford: Oxford University Press, 1991.

Opfell, Olga S. *King James Bible Translators.* Jefferson, N.C.: McFarland & Co, Inc., 1982.

Sheeley, Steven M., and Robert N. Nash, Jr. *The Bible in English Translation: An Essential Guide.* Nashville: Abingdon Press, 1997.

Tov, Emanuel. *Textual Criticism of the Hebrew Bible.* Minneapolis: Fortress Press, 1992.

Vance, Laurence M., *A Brief History of English Bible Translations.* Pensacola, Fla.: Vance Publications, 1993.

Westcott, B. F., and F. A. Hort. *Introduction to the New Testament in the Original Greek* (with "Notes on Select Readings"). New York: Harper and Brothers, 1882.